DIDGERIDOOS & DIDGERIDON'TS

A Brit's Guide to Moving Your Life Down Under

Vicky Gray

First published in Great Britain 2009 by www.BookShaker.com

Second edition published in Great Britain 2012 by Summertime
Publishing

Typeset in Trebuchet

Front cover image by © Serrnovik | Dreamstime.com

Other images by Annie Jones
www.funkyphotography.com.au

DISCLAIMER

For my family — here, there and above.

Praise for this book

"A superb guide to everything a Pom needs to know about this huge island! They may look the same, speak roughly the same language, drive on the same side of the road and claim to play cricket as well as us, but there's an entire minefield of potential slip-ups here in Australia. Didgeridoos and Didgeridon'ts unravels them all from tax to travel, sayings to sport and shopping to sickness. By the end of it you may even understand Aussie Rules Football....in fact, no way bro! A must read for anyone considering relocating or those who are already here"

Ben Southall, Winner 'Best Job in the World'
Island Caretaker - Queensland Tourism Ambassador

"A highly amusing and well-organised book, written by a British expat who has experienced the emotional rollercoaster of migrating to Oz first-hand. Vicky Gray's wry look at the highs and lows of building a new life Down Under offers all kinds of useful 'insider' knowledge, tips and facts. With this invaluable guide to hand, any would-be escapee will be armed and ready for that first year Down Under."

Joanne Mullen, editor
Australia & New Zealand Magazine

"Congratulations Vicky Gray. Your book combines priceless how-to advice with a wealth of real-life learnings that could save many Brits a painful experience in paradise. This book is exactly what Her Majesty ordered."

Andrea Martins, director and co-founder
www.expatwomen.com

"Don't want to stick out like a brand-new expat? Didgeridoos and Didgeridon'ts gives you the lowdown on life Down Under that you won't get anywhere else. A British expat, Vicky Gray has written an entertaining and informative book that includes diary entries, top tips, and official statistics, delivering what you really need to know about life in Australia. Whether you're thinking about relocating or just visiting, if you only read one guide, make sure it's this one!"

**Toni Summers-Hargis, author, Rules, Britannia:
An insider's guide to life in the United Kingdom**

"Vicky Gray leaves no grey areas in this solid, practical and personal how-to book on how to emigrate to Australia. With her wicked sense of humour, a real knack for noticing things and her accessible writing style, this is the only book I'd buy if I had the good fortune to be under 45 and could move there myself."

**Jo Parfitt, author of 28 books including
A Career in Your Suitcase, *www.joparfitt.com***

Acknowledgements

To all the people I have endlessly harassed and bewildered (and probably bored within an inch of their lives), I'd like to thank you enormously. For without your patience and encouragement, I doubt I would be sitting here writing out an acknowledgement page.

So, to Andrea Martins for starting me off and never failing to set me straight; Toni Hargis for her guiding light; Debbie Jenkins and Joe Gregory for being unfeasibly approachable; Jo Parfitt for being so patient; Joanne Mullen who gave me the confidence to begin; the wonderful Grahame Igglesdon for always being so kind and helpful; my amazing research assistant, Anne Elizabeth, for her prompt service; Annie Jones for her fabulous photos; and to all the government departments, education departments, real estate departments and Bondi surf lifesaving club – who gave me sound and accurate advice; also to my fantastic friends for our hilarious brainstorming sessions.

And finally to Max, Dayle, Jasmine and Brodie who constantly inspire me, even in the midst of utter chaos.

Thank you, thank you.

Contents

Foreword

The Australian government has encouraged migration since 1948 when the £10.00 Assisted Passage Scheme was introduced to repopulate Australia following the Second World War. Applicants who applied in those days had never visited Australia and were embarking on a new life with little knowledge or research other than the information provided by the Australian Government.

Today, the desire to live in Australia remains as strong as ever with lifestyle still the main push factor. Cheaper air travel has opened up Australia as a holiday destination and the working holiday scheme for 18–30 year olds has enabled many people to experience Australia firsthand before making a decision to migrate. They have been attracted by Australia's outdoor way of life, more affordable housing and living costs, stunning beaches and a climate ranging from Mediterranean to tropical.

Applicants will of course recognise that the decision of moving to Australia is not only influenced by lifestyle factors but can also be an emotional rollercoaster when leaving behind family and friends. The decision to move to Australia is still probably the biggest that you will ever have to make and it is essential that the move does not turn into an expensive nightmare due to a lack of planning. You will want to ensure that you have examined all of your options carefully and conducted meticulous research so that you can start your new life in Australia with realistic expectations in order to reap the long-term benefits of successful settlement.

Blue skies and pristine beaches may be just what you are looking for on holiday but settlement costs and job prospects will become much more meaningful as a migrant.

Vicky Gray has experienced the migration process and the research and planning that she put in place prior to her departure in 2006 has enabled her to settle successfully in Australia. Vicky, therefore, is well qualified to pass onto prospective migrants the do's and don'ts of moving to Australia and the knowledge she has gained through this experience will provide an invaluable source of information to applicants considering a move down under.

Grahame Igglesden
Director Concept Australia
MARA 9901024
MIA 3166

Introduction

Since immigrating to Australia in 2006, I have encountered the unexpected peaks and pitfalls that life in a new country can supply. Having read almost all the books available to me before we made the move to the other side of the world, I thought the transition would be easy – especially as we speak the same language and the culture is very similar.

Unfortunately there were still many situations that caused me to stop in my tracks; differences I would have been oblivious to, visiting on holiday. Initially it is highly amusing to mix up your thongs with your flip-flops and to search for Manchester in a department store (see page 96 if you're curious!) but when you want to sign the contract on a tenancy agreement and you still aren't sure why you would want a SLUG in your home, it gets a little tiresome.

Didgeridoos and Didgeridon'ts is a collection of short, personal experiences my family and I encountered during the first year of our new life down under, followed by all you need to know about avoiding uncomfortable situations, enabling you to be more relaxed and to remember all the reasons you chose Australia for your new home in the first place.

This book will also inform you of many other differences that you perhaps weren't aware of; such as the hopeless search for a bottle of wine in a supermarket, or being bulk-billed at a doctor's surgery. Situations that almost all Brits will encounter during that first year.

I have also included many invaluable translations in an entertaining and practical guide, to give you a leg up on the communication ladder. Read this, and feel confident about using words, phrases and pronunciations freely with the locals.

I aim to make fellow Brits aware of the phenomenon known as 'to and from Pom'.

Life in a land full of clear blue skies, beautiful beaches and spacious living isn't always utopian, especially when you are feeling homesick and all you want is a bacon butty and a pint of ale. But getting through that first year of highs and lows is vital; you will do it, but you will need all the help you can get.

I have provided a chapter of inspirational true-life stories: from people who have given up too early and gone back – only to find that their memories of their happy former life were exaggerated, and from others who have worked through homesickness and hard times and come out on the other side, relieved that they gave it a fair go.

1: Have Visa, Will Travel

For as long as I can remember I longed to live in Australia.

It started when I became obsessed by an innocent project in primary school at the age of nine. As a result, all I wanted to do was talk in an Australian accent – probably more similar to some outlandish cockney dialect – and squawk unnervingly at passers by as if I were a kookaburra.

Luckily I grew out of that and instead became a normal individual and just settled for the usual route of taking trips to discover what life was like Down Under.

I had the good fortune to meet my husband Max, who was also British but had spent many years growing up in South Australia, so once we began to have children, we decided to make the bold move once and for all and it was that one small step that led to leaps and bounds.

Getting into the Country

Having chosen Australia as the destination for your new life, you have to try and get into the country.

We have all heard the story that many, many years ago Britain sent its surplus convicts over to Australia by ship and so, as legend has it, the name POM was given to these undesirables. The story goes that this was the acronym stamped onto the backs of their uniforms and stood for Prisoner of His Majesty (POHM) or Prisoner of Mother England (POME) but this amusing anecdote is probably only an invention. Not only are there no images or examples of these uniforms, but the name 'Pom' has been recorded as far back as 1915 and further research shows that acronyms dating before the mid-twentieth century are automatically suspicious.

Anyway, if it were true, they were the lucky ones, because applying for and getting a visa takes time and money.

There are dozens of different visa classes; it all depends on your circumstances, but even the simplest application is often fraught with complex questions that need to be answered correctly and systematically to satisfy the requirements of the Department of Immigration and Citizenship (DIAC).

Therefore it is imperative that you get yourself a Migration Agent and only choose one who is registered with the Migration Agents Registration Authority (MARA). They will deal with any problems as and when they arise, quickly and professionally.

Once you have your application underway, your agent will contact you at various intervals to request information crucial to your application. One section of the visa is to have your police/character checks and a full medical check-up. The police checks cause no problems; these are easily obtained from your local constabulary at a nominal cost and they normally take a few weeks to process – unless you have a seedy criminal past, when the process may take a little longer.

The medical checks are, however, a bit more of an ordeal – or at least they were for me.

> The requirement at my time of application was for all family members to obtain a full medical examination and anyone over the age of 16 to supply a chest x-ray, which is screened to make sure you aren't carrying tuberculosis into their wondrous country. This has to be done privately, and with a doctor registered to do this sort of thing, who

you will be able to find by contacting your local GP. If there are no problems with them, the results are then forwarded to Canberra for processing.

Our application was going extremely smoothly, until about a week after we had gone for the medical checks. It was early one Friday morning, when we were frantically leaving the house for work and school, with the usual lost shoe/missing keys/something-in-eye routine, when the telephone rang. Usually I would have left it, but as we were waiting for news on the house sale etc, I hastily picked it up. It was the doctor's surgery. The doctor's grave voice made my heart race as he carefully chose his words to notify me of a slight problem with one of the blood test results.

He told me that one of the tests they had run for hepatitis C had come back with a 'false positive' result. Ever optimistic, I said,

"Surely false positive actually means 'negative'?"

Apparently not, he told me, and they would have to re-do the tests, which would take at least another week.

I think if he hadn't used such an undertaker's tone, I would certainly not have worried so. Max was still waiting in the car, revving impatiently, so I ran out to tell him of the disastrous news. Of course, he was completely confident that the test would come back perfectly normal next time and that someone had just made a cock-up, but when I went to kiss him goodbye, there was a definite hesitation. This initially made me laugh out loud as I thought he was kidding, but then it made me question his confidence.

The worst possible thing I could have done when I got back home, was scour the internet to find out how or why

I could have contracted such a disease. I hadn't shared needles during a drug-taking frenzy; I wasn't covered from head to toe in tattoos; I hadn't spent my twenties copulating with whomever I brushed past. But I did work as a dental surgery assistant for almost ten years and had sustained one minor needle stick injury.

That was it. Having read that, I was convinced I had hepatitis C and now, not only could we not fulfil our dream of moving to Australia as they would certainly not allow someone with an infectious disease in their country, I could no longer carry on working as a chiropodist in case I passed it on to my patients. Moreover, I was going to die, horribly.

To make matters worse, the result of the x-ray had come back with signs of 'plural tags'. So now I had even more reason to believe I was destined to die at any moment. You see, when I had studied chiropody, I only had to really concentrate on the lower limbs so I had just a basic knowledge of anatomy and physiology, and as we all know, a little knowledge is a dangerous thing.

Fortunately, after a discussion with a radiographer, I realised that these 'tags' were in fact completely normal and I wasn't going to die from them. So that was a relief. Now I only had hepatitis C.

Three weeks later, after constant phone calls to the surgery, I got the all-clear result. I was in no way a carrier of any disease and I was actually as fit as a butcher's dog. I thanked them for keeping the suspense going for so long, and called Max who was just as relieved as I was, now that normal relations could resume.

The visa we applied for was in the Special Migration section, as Max had spent at least nine out of 18 of his formative years in Australia.

This helped immensely, as we didn't have to go through the points-scoring test. It also helped keep the cost down.

When we looked into applying, I was unaware that there were so many visa classes – and actually how difficult it was to get into Australia, so my humble advice now is to just seek professional help and let the experts take over.

FACT
Of Australia's population of 22 million, a staggering 19% were born in the United Kingdom!

Visa Agents

The agent we used was *Concept Australia* and they offer an excellent service. They don't charge a fee for inital consultations and their advice to assess your eligibility is free and without obligation – which is fantastic, as the whole visa process can be both daunting and exhausting.

Australia has more than 140 visa classes to choose from and deciding which pathway offers you the best option can be complex as well as confusing. All of the visa classes have different assessment criteria, ranging from skilled migration to family migration and employer migration – to mention but a few.

Since the criterion is ever-changing, I will refrain from entering dozens of pages of information that will no doubt be void again before this goes to print. I will, instead give you a basic overview of the points scoring test, which seems to remain steady and a brief outline of the General Skilled Migration class.

Scoring those valuable points

The emphasis is on encouraging applicants aged 18 – 39 and who are highly skilled, speak superior English and can demonstrate significant work experience. Also, applicants who have studied and worked in Australia will also benefit from changes to the points test.

Most applicants applying from the UK will need to rely on scoring points for age, English, work experience, qualifications and sponsorship from a state or territory government or a close relative residing in regional Australia in order to reach the pass mark of 65 points.

Proposed General Skilled Migration Points Pass mark 65	Points
Age	
25-32	30
18-24 or 33-39	25
40-44	15
45-49	0
English Languge	
Competent English (IELTS 6)	0
Proficient English (IELTS 7)10	10
Superior English (IELTS 8)	20
Australian Employment	
1 year in the past 2	05
3 years in the past 5	10
5 years in the past 7	15
Overseas Employment	
3 years in the past 5	05
5 years in the past 7	10
8 years in the past 10	15
Education	
Australian or oversease PhD	20
Australian or overseas Ba or Ba + Ma/Honours	15
Australian Diploma or AQF 111/1V	10
Offshore apprenticeship	10
Other points	
Designated area sponsorship from a relative	10
State or Territory Nomination	05
Australian study requirement	05
Community Language skills	05
Regional study	05
Partner skills	05
Professional year	05

Skilled Occupations List (SOL)

The section that follows often refers to the *Skilled Occupations List*. This list is different in each state or territory, *plus* it changes regularly. Each list is broken into schedules (e.g. Schedule 1, Schedule 2 etc), which the occupations are classed into, depending on the demand for the particular skill.

As you can imagine, this information is dozens and dozens of pages long, and as I'm offering just a snippit of this highly specialised area, my advice is to jump on the internet to find out the *current* Skilled Occupations List in the state or territory you are thinking of moving to, that way you will have up-to-the-minute information and we can save a tree.

General Skilled Migration (GSM)

The GSM program comprises of three main visa subclasses.

All applicants are subject to the following mandatory assessment criteria in order to be granted a visa:

Positive skills assessment from nominated occupation on either schedules 1 or 2 of the Skilled Occupations List.

At least 12 months work experience in skilled employment highly relevant to nominated occupation for 12 out of 24 months immediately before application lodged with Department of Immigration and Citizenship (DIAC).

Must score at least 65 points. Most applicants will need to rely on points being allocated for age, English, qualifications, work experience and sponsorship in order to meet the current pass mark of 65 points.

Applicant must be of good health and character.

Skilled Independent – Subclass 175(Permanent)

Your nominated occupation *must* feature on schedule 1 of the Skilled Occupations List.

This is a permanent resident visa class and you can choose to live anywhere in Australia.

State Migration Plan – subclass 175 (permanent)

You can nominate an occupation from either schedule 1 or schedule 2 of the Skilled Occupations List

The State Migration Plan (SMP) has been developed by the states and territories to encourage applicants whose skills are recognised and in demand in their specific regions to apply for sponsorship.

Applying for sponsorship under the SMP shows a commitment to live and work in the state or territory that has sponsored you for your first two years in Australia. Each state and territory has published individual skills lists based on employment opportunities in their respective regions and has established individual criteria for work specialisations and experience as well as English language ability.

Generally you will need to show that you have a desire to live and work in the sponsoring state or territory and that you have personally undertaken research to demonstrate your knowledge and reasons for choosing the state or territory as a settlement location. Other factors that will be taken into consideration are close ties with family and friends, previous visits to the state/territory or positive interest from an employer.

Family Sponsored – subclass 176 (permanent)

Your nominated occupation *must* feature on schedule 1 of the Skilled Occupations List.

You or your partner will need to arrange sponsorship by a close relative resident in Australia and must be related to your sponsor as:

- A non-dependent child or step child
- A parent or step-parent
- A brother or sister, step-brother or sister
- A niece or nephew, step-niece or step-nephew
- An aunt or uncle, step-aunt or uncle

Please note that no points are awarded for sponsorship.

State Migration Plan – subclass 475 (provisional)

You can nominate an occupation from either schedule 1 or schedule 2 of the Skilled Occupations List.

This visa subclass has similar characteristics to SMP subclass 176 but is provisional with emphasis on you residing in a regional or low growth area (defined by post code) of the state or territory that has sponsored you.

The visa is valid for three years with an option to apply for a permanent visa providing you have resided in a specified regional area of Australia for two years and worked full-time in an occupation on the SOL (schedules 1 or 2) for one year.

You will be required to sign an undertaking that you, and any secondary applicants included in your application, will live, work or study, in a regional or a low population growth metropolitan area in Australia, gazetted at the time your provisional visa was granted for the duration of your visa.

GSM Family Sponsorship – subclass 475 (provisional)

Your nominated occupation *must* feature on schedule 1 of the Skilled Occupations List.

This visa subclass is provisional and valid for three years with an option to apply for a permanent visa providing you have resided in a designated area of Australia (defined by post code) for two years and worked full-time in an occupation on schedule 1 of the SOL for one year.

You or your partner must arrange sponsorship by a relative who has resided in a designated area of Australia (defined by postcode) for a minimum of 12 months prior to the lodgement of your application.

You or your partner must be related to your sponsor as:

- A non-dependent child or step child
- A parent or step-parent
- A brother or sister, step-brother or sister
- A niece or nephew, step-niece or step-nephew
- An aunt or uncle, step-aunt or uncle
- Grandparent or step-grandparent
- 1st cousin

It can be an expensive procedure and at times, you wonder what on earth you are doing it for. I mean, Great Britain isn't all *that* bad. And if you were to take away the grim weather, the traffic congestion, over-population and crammed-in new housing estates, the difference between both countries wouldn't be so noticeable. Really? Do read on!

Resources

Visa Agents

www.conceptaustralia.co.uk
www.emigrationgroup.co.uk
www.thinkingaustralia.com
www.overseas-emigration.co.uk

TOP TIP

You could scour the internet for hours looking
for an appropriate agent, but just remember
that you may have to go in person to their office,
so check where that is located first.

2: One Small Step

"Pack your bags – you're moving to Australia!"

The long-awaited phone call from the estate agent finally came, just as I had been gawping mindlessly out of the bedroom window at the dense February grey clouds.

The agent and his enthusiastic team had taken over marketing our house when we were horribly let down eight months earlier: our previous buyers had pulled out at the eleventh hour. We had already provisionally sold my chiropody business; Max's hairdressing salon; lined up purchasers for our cars and endured various Sunday morning car boot sales at 5am in arctic conditions. To top it all I had given away most of my winter woollies to dear, but vulture-like, friends. After months of my persistent badgering, I could only imagine his joy at finally removing our house details from his window display. I, on the other hand, had been here before and wasn't terribly convinced by his eagerness.

But once I'd hung up, having gone through all the routine solicitor number swapping, I slumped down onto my eight-year-old son's bed, stunned. The couple who had viewed the house wanted to move in – and fast: in eight weeks to be precise.

Of course anyone who has bought or sold a property in England will know how impossible that sounds. I began to feel overwhelmed by the excitement and magnitude of it all. So as I stood up and glanced back out of the window, this time to behold a magnificent blue sky with threads of wispy clouds, I pulled myself together, for this – I proclaimed – was the first step towards our new life Down

Under!

Remarkably, it was precisely eight weeks later that we moved out.

By the time the day came, we were both barely conscious after our leaving do the evening before. It wasn't stupidity that caused us to have our party the day before we moved, it was just that the date for the move had been brought forward and we hadn't been able to change the party.

Unfortunately, the move did not go quite as smoothly as I had wished. The new owners were scheduled to arrive with their removal van at noon. Luckily, the main international movers had been and taken all our furniture to be shipped over to Brisbane earlier that week, leaving us with only basics to pack into a reasonably sized transit van, which we were driving up to my mum's house in the Wirral, That's where we were staying for the next month or so, tying up the last bits of never-ending paperwork.

My terribly organised, but ever-so-ham-handed sister had come down from Merseyside for the party and to help us move. She and her teenage daughter managed to compress (and break) the last of our worldly belongings, squeezing them into the already creaking van. We meanwhile dealt with other pressing matters, like finalising completion on Max's hairdressing salon – another task that could only be done on that specific day – just to add to the chaos.

Due to a lack of communication with the estate agent, and probably a lack of intelligible mumblings on my behalf, the new owners had got the call to start proceedings and had eagerly raced to their new abode, an hour earlier than we expected them.

What a sight that greeted them – it was rather different from the serene house I had dutifully shown them round a couple of months earlier.

There were half deflated-airbeds with unzipped sleeping bags all around the house and sponge bags spilling out flannels and hangover remedies onto the floor, There were wet towels strewn over the banisters, McDonald's muffin wrappers and disposable coffee cups adorning the once impeccably shiny kitchen worktops and, to top it all, bags with half bottles of Imperial vodka poking out. I couldn't have made a worse impression if I had tried!

With a blushing, slightly sweaty face and a mouth that felt like I had swallowed a leather upper, I apologetically started to shove the last few items into the van, unconvincingly reassuring them "We won't be long".

A few crashes and quick slamming of doors later, we were done. The woman eagerly accepted my keys with a pitying smile, and we trundled off in a convoy.

An hour up the M1, what we had just done suddenly hit me. I started to feel the first sense of panic of the realisation at what we were doing. Although I was excited about the new adventure, I felt immense sadness about leaving my safe and familiar home behind. I know that that is probably how most people feel when they leave their own homes of many years, but this time there was no 'other' house to move into, and we didn't have the vaguest idea where we were even going to start searching.

Was this the beginning of the homesickness that everybody had warned me about?

Navigating Your Knick-Knacks

As customs and quarantine are so tight, heavy penalties apply if you deliberately break the rules. This can be very inconvenient and costly so DON'T do it! You could find out how to apply for the relevant permits yourself, but probably the best way to ensure that you get your goods to Australia without too many problems is to use an international removal company.

TOP TIP

When choosing your removal company, it is their job to deal with customs clearance, permits and other documentation, but do make sure that the price for this is included in your quote.

Whether you decide to deal with permits yourself or use a removal company, you will be required to complete an Unaccompanied Personal Effects statement; this is to ensure that travellers comply with Australian customs, quarantine, wildlife and currency laws. It has about eight sections and it's fairly easy to fill in, so it isn't too much of a drama.

Many people have contacted me wondering what furniture I brought over; did I, for example, have a full container, or just a half? As some of the furniture we owned was a little on the tired side, we narrowed it down and brought just the most desirable articles. We decided that we would ship over our rather rustic dining room furniture, our settee, some odds and ends from the kitchen, our clothes and about 20 or so tea chests full of children's toys.

Of course, when it actually came down to it, we ended up taking far more stuff than we thought – and so will you! Like the boxes of photos you have accumulated and the hoards of wedding/new baby cards you simply can't get rid of due to sentimental value and then there's that easel you inherited from great-aunt Constance.

You must be either really ruthless or at least extremely realistic. Then when the international removal men come and give you a quote, they will be able to have a good idea what size container you are going to need – leaving you with no nasty surprises on the day.

What Not to Take

We decided against bringing over many electrical items such as televisions as they really don't travel well, especially the delicate plasma types. Besides, they are becoming more affordable than ever now. Even the one we bought when we arrived has come down significantly in price.

We left behind microwave ovens and vacuum cleaners. I did this because I didn't want to have dozens of adapters on all my electrical equipment. However, I have since found out that you can easily change your UK plugs over to Aussie ones for a mere $3 at Bunnings Warehouse (like B&Q). This is quite easy to do and will save you battling with adapters. It often becomes awkward if you need to plug in two items in the same double plug socket as the adapters are cumbersome and it is difficult to squeeze another plug (even a slightly smaller Australian one) next to it. It's not the end of the world, but bothersome so worth mentioning.

DVD players are a difficult one. Some are 'region free', which means they will play any DVD from either country (Australia is region 4, UK is region 2). But other DVD players may not play Australian DVDs – even though Australia has the same electrical voltage (240v). If in doubt, Google your DVD model number – you may find the solution is as simple as keying in some codes into your remote control. Check out the resources page for more information.

One item I long for, and foolishly left behind, was my tumble dryer.

About a year before we left I had bought a new condenser model, but as we had made the decision to leave electrical appliances behind, I gave it away. If I had realised that tumble dryers were so vital due to the humid wet season of January and February, I would certainly not have been so generous.

I now have a very basic machine, a rather steamy laundry room and very curly hair.

```
┌─────────────────────────────────────────────┐
│                  TOP TIP                      │
│  It is near impossible to buy a condenser     │
│  tumble dryer without paying the earth, so    │
│  if you have one already in the UK, bring     │
│  it over.                                      │
└─────────────────────────────────────────────┘
```

Fridges have recently become a new issue. Due to CFC emissions there has been new legislation about ozone protection. Check with your removal company if you are considering bringing yours over in case your model doesn't comply with regulations.

Declare or Beware

Food, plants or animal products brought from overseas could cause devastating results to Australia's unique environment, so it is taken extremely seriously. The motto is: DECLARE OR BEWARE!

What follows here, are some of the items that you must declare on arrival. In many cases, items you declare will be returned to you after inspection. Some may be allowed in if accompanied by an import permit – issued by the Australian Quarantine and Inspection Service (AQIS) prior to arrival, or with treatment in Australia to make them safe (fees and charges apply). Alternatively, you can drop them in quarantine bins at the airport.

Foodstuffs

- any type of food, dried fruit
- herbs and spices
- instant noodles
- rice
- biscuits
- cakes and confectionery
- black tea, coffee or any other beverages
- packaged meals
- snack foods, even infant formula (unless accompanied by an infant)
- anything dairy or egg-related
- fresh or powdered milk
- cheese or non-dairy creamers
- any products that contain either 10% dairy or 10% egg, such as mayonnaise or any homemade egg products, including noodles and pasta that are not commercially manufactured
- any animal product including all uncanned meat, fresh, dried, frozen, cooked, smoked or preserved – from all animal species
- pet food, including canned products
- fish and other seafood
- sandwiches containing meat
- any seeds or nuts
- cereal grain
- raw nuts
- popping corn
- pine cones

- birdseed or even ornaments containing seeds
- fresh and frozen fruit or vegetables

Animal Products

- feathers
- bones or horns
- wool or animal hair
- skins or furs
- shells or coral – even jewellery
- bee products – including honey, beeswax and honeycomb
- stuffed animals and birds (taxidermy certificate required)
- any animal equipment including saddlery and tack and animal or birdcages

Plant Material

- bare rooted plants
- plant cuttings
- bulbs or stems
- souvenirs made of straw
- wooden articles and carvings
- items that include bark
- bamboo, cane or rattan basket ware
- mats, bags or anything else made from plant material
- dried flowers and arrangements
- pot pourri and coconut shells and definitely no Christmas decorations like wreaths, dried holly, conifer items or blown eggs (I know of many families who have had theirs confiscated).

Other Goods

Craft and hobby lines made from animal or plant material will not be allowed. Also your bicycles, footwear, sporting and camping equipment, hiking boots and golf clubs all need to be free from soil contamination.

Because there is also a risk that the freshwater algae didymo could enter, make sure fishing rods and nets, waders, kayaks, paddles and life jackets are all thoroughly cleaned and dry.

Quarantine officers will still want to send the equipment for treatment to make sure it is safe.

Even when you are on the aircraft, you will be required to fill out an Incoming Passenger Card, which is a legal document. You must tick YES to declare if you are carrying any food, plant material or animal products.

On arrival your baggage may be x-rayed or checked by a dog detector team, so if you fail to declare any items you could be in *big trouble*.

TOP TIP
For more information about items of quarantine concern and other frequently asked questions check out the government website:
www.daff.gov.au/aqis/faqs

You could be fined $220 on the spot; or in extreme cases prosecuted and fined more than $60,000 and risk 10 years in jail if you haven't declared certain items.

But you *will not be penalised* if goods are declared, so just to reiterate, declare *everything*, even that tube of Smarties in your son's Spider-Man bag.

One last point, if you have any of those items listed and you really can't bear to be parted from them, you can always apply for a special permit. The quarantine officials may be able to offer some type of treatment to make it safe, for example fumigation or irradiation.

Resources

Removals

www.anglopacific.co.uk
www.pssremovals.com
www.johnmason.com

Information on DVD Conversions

www.regionfreedvd.net

Official Quarantine Information

www.aqis.gov.au

3: Pets on Planes

Taking animals overseas is not a decision to make lightly. I was all for leaving my two cats in a nice loving home in England, maybe with a lonely elderly lady in a cosy little bungalow full of unusual nooks and crannies, homemade knitted blankets draped around precariously and a two-bar electric heater permanently on through all seasons.

But when it came down to it, I couldn't leave my moggies behind. They may have been old and ragged – in particular my male cat who resembled a threadbare cushion, had half an ear missing, a cataract and a surplus undercarriage – but they were my responsibility and for that reason, I decided to take them with me to live out their twilight years in a place in the sun.

We had arranged for a pet shipping company to take charge of the shipping of our beloved cats. As it had been quite late notice for the company, I had to hang on to them until the day we were moving out, so I had made it very clear to my sister and the children not to enter the utility room where our imprisoned and mystified animals, Aubrey and Fluffer, were.

The chap arrived promptly at 10 am in the specially designed, pet-friendly van to get them started on their voyage to a life of constant sun and fun-filled retirement pleasures.

After more paperwork and proof of inoculations etc, we managed to get Aubrey safely and securely placed into his adequately large and comfy transit cage...

Fluffer, on the other hand, a timid and normally obliging animal, turned into a feral, froth-mouthed maniac and bolted towards the street door and into the woods to the side of our house in a cloud of fur, spray and dust.

I resisted panic, even though we had less than two hours before the new owners arrived. I went into the kitchen trying to look as calm as possible and re-opened an already sealed box labelled 'kitchen stuff' and grabbed a tin of tuna – Fluffer's vice. The cat transport chap nodded his head accordingly, as though he'd seen this a thousand times and I proceeded to open the tin...

Instinctively, I pulled open a now completely empty kitchen drawer, which normally housed all our utensils, but of course all of these were on a container somewhere south of Europe, not to be seen again for three months.

My expression, up until now, had resembled a slightly bewildered clown, but at this point it became a grimace of horror. I turned to the man, and made a feeble attempt to laugh. He was looking less patient than before and glanced slyly at his watch.

"Emma!" I yelled, darting outside and towards the house next door, tuna in hand. My neighbour was always very obliging with the loan of household objects and I knew she would be able to help – but to my dismay, her car was not in the drive.

Clutching at straws I decided to knock anyway, on the off chance her husband had taken the car and she was sitting there serenely, with a kitchen drawer full of can openers in assorted colours, just for my convenience.

Instead of Emma, an unfamiliar mastic-stained workman answered the door, which made my ever-hopeful expression wither, but as the door was open and time was of the essence, I had no choice but to blurt out an explanation as to why I had to immediately intrude the kitchen and rummage irrationally through the kitchen drawers. The poor chap said nothing, but watched in amazement as I tornadoed frantically around the room. Eventually, at the bottom of a dark corner, I spied a tin-opener, ancient and hazardously rusty, but it was damn well going to do the trick. I battled desperately with it, as slimy drips of brine dribbled down my arm to my elbow, then I dropped it in the sink and bolted out the door shouting,

"Thanks! Tell her it was Vicky. She'll understand."

The man stood silently watching, mouth agape.

Max had already scaled the six-foot fence to the woods, so all I could see was a pair of hands, clapping to attract my attention to give him the dripping can of tuna. I watched through a knot in the fence as he carefully manoeuvred around the randomly dotted dog dirt to the target. Poor brainless Fluffer fell immediately for the trap and after a few mouthfuls of tuna was whipped up and whisked over towards my beckoning hands. After a further struggle and a rather insincere attempt at an apology, she was safely parcelled up next to her brother, who was looking at her in utter disgust... and then off they went to the Great Southern Land.

Choosing a Pet Shipping Company

Your first impression may be that it is rather a performance to take your animals overseas, especially when you have so many other matters to attend to, but help is at hand. The professional companies that organise your beloved pets take over the burden of quarantine permits, documentation etc, so don't be too disheartened.

As Australia is free of many animal-related diseases found around the world, AQIS (Australian Quarantine and Inspection Service) stick to strict guidelines. So when you are looking to ship over your furry friends, check that the shipping company can organise:

- flights, documentation and veterinary requirements
- boarding and grooming
- a collection service to wherever you live
- delivery to the airport and their final spray, worm and health certificate.

Another important factor is to ensure the comfort of your pet. Ask if the air kennels they use for transit are approved by the IATA (International Air Transport Association). This ensures that they meet a certain construction criteria and will put your mind at rest about the animal's travelling safety and comfort. They will have adequate ventilation for the animal and will be 'nose and paw proof', which conjured up many distressing images.

Vaccinations and Requirements

All animals entering Australia *must* have an import permit prior to shipment and have a microchip which is compatible with Avid, Destron, Trovan or any other ISO compatible reader. Your shipping company will have a list of approved veterinary surgeons in your local area, so you can hold their paw whilst they receive this little requirement.

Immunisations do change periodically, but generally the rule is that dogs must be fully vaccinated against distemper, hepatitis, parvovirus, parainfluenza and kennel cough. A few blood tests are thrown in for good measure and the results should show a *negative* reading for leptospirosis, so ensure the vet doesn't give a full booster, as that will be included in the vaccination.

Vaccination and blood test certificates must accompany the animals during shipment.

Cats get a better deal and only have to have vaccinations against feline enteritis, feline rhinotracheitis and feline calicivirus. Both dogs and cats must be vaccinated at least 14 days before the flight (and not more than 11 months before) and they must be sprayed and wormed within a specified time of travelling.

How are we going so far? Still want to bring them along?

Quarantine Matters

Departures

Animals will not be fed prior to departure, in case they soil their quarters, which are all equipped with water containers, regularly refilled during transit. At least they don't have to endure airline food!

Make sure your pet has a place at your nominated quarantine station on arrival – having an import permit does not guarantee a space.

Your shipping company should have made that arrangement separately, as the quarantine stations get extremely booked up at certain times of the year, so if they haven't pre-booked a bed, there might just be no room at the inn.

Arrivals

Once their Aussie adventure has begun and touchdown has occurred, they will have a thorough veterinary check and will then be transported to their new halls of residence at the quarantine station.

Although AQIS do not allow you to visit your precious pets on the day of their arrival, you can visit and interact with them during their stay. Visiting hours vary, so check with your station. All animals must complete a 30-day quarantine stay and facilities are located in Sydney, Melbourne and Perth. Arrangements can be made by your shipping company to transport them to the other states, once their 30-day sentence is complete. They do not get out early for good behaviour.

So Go On... How Much?

When it comes down to it, no matter how much you would love your pets to travel with you on your new adventure, the big question is price. So to help you make your decision clearer here are *approximate* prices (in Aussie dollars).

Import permits from DEFRA (Department for Environment, Food and Rural Affairs) in Canberra are $325 plus $165 for each additional animal. Payments can be lodged electronically or faxed/posted with card payment details. Note that the cost is increased if you lodge the forms manually, so it's probably financially advantageous to do it from the website:

http://www.daff.gov.au/aqis/cat-dogs/application

Make sure your animal is microchipped *before* you apply.

One application form is needed per animal and the permit is valid for six months. You also need the permit before you can book their space in the quarantine station.

Here are some approximate pet-related costs (in sterling) to consider:

Boarding/day (cat)	£14 (£21 for 2 cats if second cat is sharing)
Boarding/day (dog)	£18 (£27 for 2 dogs if second dog is sharing)
Flight per cat – depends on level of service you require	£700–£1,000
Flight per dog – depends on size/weight of dog and level of service you require	£1,100–£2,800

There are also the vet fees for having the vaccinations, microchipping, spraying/worming and a Health Certificate needs to be obtained. Also, always allow for other minor fees that may crop up, such as collection of your pet to the shipping company's headquarters and the boxes of tissues you'll get through when you wave them off!

The following prices are all in Aussie dollars, as they relate to arrival in Australia.

Quarantine entry fee (per animal)	$15
Dog – daily rate for accommodation	$39
Subsequent dog if sharing accommodation	$33
Cat – daily rate for accommodation	$29
Subsequent cat if sharing accommodation	$23
Document clearance (add $40 per 15 mins if additional information is required.)	$40
Veterinary examination per animal (charged per 15 mins, usually 30 mins is required)	$40 (x2)
Please note: Additional veterinary care (such as booster vaccinations) will be charged to the owner by private veterinarian	

If you need to have your pet flown to another airport (Brisbane, Darwin, Canberra or Adelaide), the costs can vary once again, depending on the size/weight of the animal. For cats, it's somewhere in the region of $250.

ODD SPOT

Something I read at the foot of my shipping confirmation document – and found unnerving – was that my cats had a customs value of just £20.
What? Was that all?!

Made Up Your Mind?

Alas, after only 18 months of living in Australia, both of my cherished cats had passed away. Although they were not bitten by snakes or hunted down by a pack of wild dingoes... one did fall prey to an incident that could definitely have been avoided... if I'd read this book! (see page 127) while the other fell peacefully asleep under the shade of a swaying palm tree.

But I could never have left them behind, even if I had managed to find a sweet – and slightly blind – elderly lady without high cat standards!

Resources

Transporting Pets to Australia

www.petexports.co.uk
www.shepherdhillkennels.com

Quarantine Station Addresses

Sydney
Eastern Creek Animal Quarantine Station
60 Wallgrove Road
Eastern Creek, NSW 2766
easterncreek.aqs@aquis.gov.au

Melbourne
Spotswood Animal Quarantine Station
PO Box 1079
Newport, Victoria 3051
spotswood.quarantine@aquis.gov.au

Perth
Byford Animal Quarantine Station
PO Box 61
Byford, WA 6122
byfordq@aquis.gov.au

Transporting Pets Around Australia

www.jetpets.com.au
www.pettransport.com.au
www.animaltransport.com.au
www.animaltravel.com.au

4: Goodbye Blighty

We still had many loose ends to tie up with insurance (including retrieving no-claim bonuses for car insurance), bank accounts (closing British ones and opening Aussie ones) and final tax payments.

So we were grateful to have another month in the UK staying at my mum's, whose house is big enough to accommodate us comfortably, crushed furniture and all.

The month whizzed by, but it wasn't long before conversations started along the lines of, "what are you going to do when you get back?" and "when it's out of your system, will you be moving up here, or staying in Essex?"

I realised I was making the right decision to go out on a limb and have our Big Adventure. I knew they meant well, so I tried hard not to breathe out in a tiresome manner.

The day came when we had to say goodbye to the family, and I kid you not, no matter how bad you think this part is going to be, it is always much, much worse.

Firstly, you have to try and remain calm, which is not an easy task when your brain is pulsing into overdrive to make sure you have every last item on your inventory. Forgetting something now really matters.

Then you have the physical aspect to try and disguise: the cold sweats, the nausea churning away in the pit of your stomach, the heart palpitations that cause you to gyrate slightly if you keep still and finally, that bizarre nervous stretching thing that happens to people when they are about to do something uncomfortable.

You have no idea when you are going to see your beloved family and friends again, and soon they will no longer be able to relate to your day-to-day life. Remember – you're going it alone.

And so with that, you hug each one of them, with such affection that you could cause mild respiratory problems, and then slump hopelessly into the cab, sobbing uncontrollably.

Now, cab drivers mean well, and it is not their intention to be irritating, but is it not obvious that sometimes people don't want to converse?

We were emigrating, not popping to Spain for a couple of weeks, and I was probably not going to see my nephews until they were old enough to worry about using hair implants.

I couldn't have cared less who was going into the jungle for Celebrity Get Me Out of Here but he wanted to share gossip about this and every other reality show on television. He droned on and on and I did my best not to listen.

Thankfully, there were no road works of any substance on our journey and we got to Manchester airport with plenty of time to spare. It had started raining and as I looked around at the grey skies, I felt a jitter of excitement at the prospect at what lay ahead.

We checked our oversized luggage in at the appropriate check-in counter. Would we ever see it again? The girl's vagueness about the need to recheck at Singapore was not reassuring. We made a mental note that we would have a look when we got there to see if it was going straight to our first destination of Adelaide, just to be safe.

Blow the Bamboozlement of Banking

Before we took the plunge we did our research. We had attended a number of exhibitions to get information on finding out where to live to get the best from our chosen Aussie lifestyle.

We investigated opening bank accounts, changing over sterling to dollars (including the right time to do so), plus loads of other information that these places are just jam-packed with.

There are four main Australia-wide banks (also known as the 'big four'):
- ANZ Bank
- Commonwealth Bank
- National Australia Bank (NAB)
- Westpac Banking Corporation

There are also some state-wide banks:

- Bank of Queensland (mainly Queensland)
- Suncorp (Queensland)
- HSBC
- St George Bank
- Bankwest (Western Australia)
- Citibank
- Home Building Society (Western Australia)

Before we arrived in Australia, we had already organised our bank accounts. We had been steered in the direction of the Commonwealth Bank of Australia by our migration agent, and as we had no other knowledge of Australian banks decided that would be perfectly suitable. Their office was based in London so we made a weekend break of it, taking in the sights from the London Eye; exploring the Tower of London and generally meandering enthusiastically. We enjoyed ourselves enormously and ignored the cool drizzle that March can often bring, although we were gratified to peel off our sodden socks in the comfort of the hotel room every evening.

Bank Charges

The staff at the Commonwealth Bank of Australia (CBA) were exceptionally helpful. They guided us through the different accounts available and which would suit us, and also informed us of the bank charges. This seemed to us completely archaic as these charges certainly are not imposed in UK banks any more.

The average Australian still pays bank charges for the luxury of having a regular current account. You can pay a low, flat monthly fee by having a *streamline* account (which gives you unlimited access to your money) for around $6.

On other accounts, you can use the ATM machines only a specified number of times before you get charged. It costs you to use assisted withdrawals over the counter, write cheques and negotiate them through the clearing system and also if you use an ATM which is not one belonging to the Commonwealth Bank.

Some other information that was quite important was that within six weeks of arrival in Australia, you must take yourselves along to the branch where you have your account in order to identify yourselves with your passports.

They will require a contact address. If you are staying in short-term accommodation you can give them that – you don't need to provide any further proof of address.

At some point you will need to apply for a tax file number (TFN), so that your interest is paid without tax being deducted. You can apply for a TFN online, but I will address this later in the book.

TOP TIP
If you open a bank account with the Commonwealth Bank at the UK branch in London before you leave, they usually offer to waive the fees as they understand personal banking in the UK is free. Most Australians I have spoken to do incur fees on their bank accounts and are quite disgusted when they realise that this is not the case in other countries.

Transferring Money

Another question we had was how we could transfer large sums of money to Australia and get the best possible exchange rate. The CBA told us of a company called HIFX, a financial services company which specialises in foreign currency exchange.

HIFX is able to give you all the help and advice you need to save money on all your international money transfers and protects your money from fluctuating exchange rates. HIFX offers better exchange rates than your bank.

While I listened to Max and the well-informed bank clerk drone on, I started to glaze over as I normally do when figures are being discussed. I tried to stifle my yawns, until an article in one of the Australian newspapers caught my eye.

Not wishing to appear rude or bored, I carried on nodding in occasional agreement. Once the formalities were over, I asked if I could perhaps keep the newspaper I had been secretly reading.

The article I had been drawn to turned out to be invaluable to our migratory experience, for this is where I found out about a company called Brisbane Bound, which offers short-term accommodation for Brits in Brisbane. I have included all the details of this service later in this book, and it is well worth looking into if you are emigrating with a family.

Resources

Banks

Commonwealth Bank of Australia
www.commbank.com.au (for up-to-date information on bank charges, go to 'personal', then 'bank accounts' and click on the comparison table in the sidebar).

Their address in London is:

Senator House
85 Queen Victoria Street
London
EC4V 4HA
Tel: (+44) 020 7710 3990
www.migrantbanking.co.uk

ANZ Bank
40 Bank Street
Canary Wharf
London
E14 5EJ
Tel: (+44) 020 3229 2121
www.anz.com.au

Westpac Banking Corporation
Contact the migrant banking team on (+44) 020 7621 7000 or email: ukmigrantbanking@westpac.com.au.
www.westpac.com.au

National Australia Bank (NAB) – Migrant Banking
NAB Migrant Banking Centre
4th floor
Gateway House
Richmond
TW9 1DN
Tel: (+44) 020 8614 9320
Email: migrant.banking@eu.nabgroup.com
www.nabgroup.com/migrantbanking

NAB provided the following comment, especially for use in this book: "Helping you move to Australia, our dedicated migrant banking team can help you set up your business and personal banking requirements before you touch down in Australia. When you arrive, you will have your own banking manager to help you with your financial needs – whether it's a home loan, credit cards or business banking needs."

Money Transfers
www.hifx.co.uk
www.tranzmoney.com
www.foreign-currency.com

5: Encountering Oz

We had visited Adelaide a few years earlier, so we were very familiar with my mother-in-law's modest 1845 cottage. Although compact, it had running water, some obscure cooking facilities and a place where one could bathe and use the lavatory – thankfully indoors. Of course, when we last visited it was just coming to the end of summer, so the temperature was glorious.

This time we had arrived in early winter – a completely different story. Outside it was sunny, maybe a little fresh first thing in the morning, but still wonderful compared to the harsh British winters. Unfortunately the interior of the cottage (a term I use loosely) proved to be a darkened pit of despair.

I can honestly say that I have never encountered such cold, damp dismal conditions. That is, aside from a New Year's Hogmanay in Dundee many, many years before, where I spent the evening and the wee hours wringing wet with rain-saturated clothing before collapsing onto an equally soggy bed in some high-rise, narrowly escaping pneumonia.

Now I don't want to appear ungrateful. I am lucky to have a fantastic mother-in-law whom I care for dearly, but when the outside temperature exceeds the inside enough to cause fingers to become so numb that they feel they have been plunged into liquid nitrogen, it is time to ignite some heating in the house.

After some deliberation, the gas-fired heater was turned on and we could, at last, cautiously defrost our extremities, as long as we were within a two feet radius of it.

Further away it felt as if we were living in the chilled fruit and veg section of Sainsbury's.

My mother-in-law showed us a fantastic time in Adelaide. She took us to world-famous wineries, such as the Barossa Valley, where we rummaged through unusual curios up in the hills of a little township called Harndorf. We enjoyed the sights of this fantastically well-designed city before coasting down long, vast, seemingly endless country roads to areas such as Victor Harbour and Kangaroo Island. We stopped occasionally stopping at wildlife parks for the children to pet and feed koalas and kangaroos and, of course, met up with Max's family and friends.

We had decided to stay overnight on Kangaroo Island, and had picked a quaint little motel called Wisteria Lodge. It boasted an outdoor pool and spa and was next to the beach, so once we had checked in, we went out to explore the island and its promised wildlife.

We spent endless hours driving around without getting even a sniff of the departing tail of anything still breathing. There were many corpses strewn across the roads, including huge kangaroos whose bulk must have inflicted serious damage to the vehicle that hit them. I had to avert the children's eyes from the splattered possums for fear of bloodcurdling screams and the inevitable nightmares.

The one wildlife encounter we did have was with an enormous lizard. It resembled a small scaly dinosaur and seemed to be waiting patiently for our car to pass. We stopped to get a closer look, to take a photo and maybe poke it a little, only to realise on inspection that the reason it hadn't scarpered at the sight of us was that its entire face was buried deep in an unrecognisable decapitated furry body... and so the screaming began.

Once the children were suitably consoled, we headed off to the seal sanctuary along the south of the island. We were met and promptly organised into groups by a very knowledgeable guide, and off we all shuffled along the perfect white sand to meet dozens of beautiful seals.

They were fantastic.

The guide gave us strict instructions on how to behave while we were close to them, and everyone adhered to the rules, which meant that the seals didn't feel threatened. Eventually a few of them clumsily humped their lumbering bodies over to study us. Much to my son's horror, as the memory of the earlier mutilation scene was still fresh in his mind, he instinctively shot on to Max's shoulders for sanctuary, causing a timid baby seal to snort ferociously, uncomfortably close to my left foot, leaving little pot holes in the sand.

I cautiously buried my foot deeper into the sand and gulped hard, trying not to look too frightened of this small cute creature, remembering it was after all, a wild animal and could at any moment shoot straight for the jugular. Couldn't it?

The rest of the tour went by without any further trauma. It was immensely enjoyable and informative, but it was soon time for us to head back to the motel. We had been warned by various people that we shouldn't travel about by car after nightfall, due to the number of kangaroos endlessly bounding around in the dark. More importantly, our car insurance was invalid if damage was caused by a kangaroo colliding into us during its nocturnal adventures.

Back at the motel, we all enjoyed a steamy shower and a hearty meal in the restaurant, which was mainly occupied by warm, smiling octogenarians who nodded warmly at our two well-behaved children.

After the meal we headed over to the beach, to gaze at the night sky, and what a beautiful sight it was! The southern hemisphere has the most dazzling array of stars I have ever encountered, and viewing them in a remote place like Kangaroo Island, where the generators switch off late in the evening, transforms the sky. No doubt it is equally captivating around the world, but when you live near a heavily populated area, where street and shop lights are forever on, there is just no way of observing it with the naked eye and getting the full force of its beauty.

Even the children were in awe as we lay on the sand, gazing at the deep black canvas above us, with no moon to dilute the impact of the billions of bright twinkling specks. We were able to count mere seconds between each of the dozens of shooting stars that darted through the sky, None of us will forget that first experience of the southern night sky.

Creature Encounters

Obviously anybody who has already decided to live in Australia will be all too aware of the many venomous spiders and snakes lurking about. Queensland alone is host to about 80 different land snakes, of which 20 are capable of inflicting a seriously damaging, if not fatal, bite to humans.

Of all the questions I have been asked since moving to Oz, the most common is about the infamous spider and snake situation, so I couldn't write this book without dedicating a chapter to the subject.

As this book is about the encounters I *personally* have had since living here, I am going to introduce you to some of the fun creatures I have actually met.

I can go for weeks, maybe months without seeing any signs of eight-legged friends, but I would be lying if I told you that I never encounter them. Since living here, I have become used to checking under the toilet seat before parking my bottom and to banging out my shoes before putting them on in the morning. I do now walk about outside barefoot without first scanning the area for anything untoward.

But every now and again, you may find yourself face to face with something you thought was only kept behind safety glass in a zoo. So, as requested by many Brits, here is a summary of creatures to avoid and some that you may *want* to welcome into your home. An unusual request, you may think, but please read on.

Encounter 1 – Huntsman Spider

There are a couple of months in winter when even the most hardened swimmers decide it is a little too chilly to have a morning dip, or for the children to swim after their homework (a great bribe – incidentally). As we have many inflatable pool toys for the children to play with, it is usual for me to pop them in the shed until the warmer weather is upon us again.

So I was quite happily going about my routine of neatly placing the deflated sharks, crocodiles and dinghies in the enormous corrugated shed at the foot of our garden, when I felt a presence. As I slowly swivelled around, a huntsman spider the size of a dinner plate was perched on its back legs with its haunches up. I have never had a problem with spiders but this made me shudder. I am aware that they are not venomous and it could cause me no actual harm, but it was so repulsive and fiendish that I bolted out of there in a split second.

I was so impressed by the size of this spider, that I contacted Australia Zoo to see if they wanted it as an exhibit. With regret they informed me that they don't have spiders at their zoo, so I was forced to keep it in my shed for the purposes of scaring guests.

There are several different varieties of huntsman spider, but all of them have one major similarity: they all terrify people by their sudden appearance, like from behind curtains or hiding behind the sun visor in your car before racing across your dashboard. Thankfully I have never experienced such an episode, and I pray it stays that way.

Huntsman spiders are extremely large, measuring on average about 15cm across, due to their long, hairy legs. They are generally found on the ground under loose bark, rocks and foliage. Some huntsman spiders are quite sociable and can, on occasions, be seen sitting together with dozens of others under bark on dead trees and stumps; not a tea party I would like to stumble upon.

The colours of these spiders vary too, but most are grey to brown and some of them have stripy legs. Flattened bodies enable them to live in narrow spaces such as rock crevices, and maybe between the CDs in your rack.

Male and female huntsman spiders have a lengthy courtship which involves mutual caresses. The male fertilises her eggs by inserting his palps into her, after he has finished drumming them against the trunk of a tree. They then live peacefully together often in large colonies. Unlike some spiders, which eat the male after mating, the ritual is all very harmonious and the male is rarely attacked.

The female then produces a flat, oval egg sac of white papery silk and lays up to 200 eggs. For three weeks after that, she stands guard over it, not even popping off for a bite to eat.

She can get pretty grouchy during this period and if she gets provoked can rear up in a defensive display, which I can relate to at certain times of the month.

Once these spiderlings have emerged, the female will stay with them for several weeks while they have their first few moults and will then move on. Their lifespan is about two years.

The bite from a huntsman usually only causes local pain and swelling, but some badge varieties have been known to cause prolonged pain, inflammation, headaches, vomiting and an irregular pulse. If you do experience problems, seek medical attention. They are not known as killers but as they do resemble tarantulas, a late night encounter with one crawling out from the inside of a toilet roll, may cause heart failure.

Encounter 2 – Spider Wasp

One afternoon as I walked quickly into the backyard to bring in my washing before Max once again scolded me for bleaching his dark T-shirts (a downside to the arid Australian sun if your washing line isn't undercover), I stopped short.

Ahead of me, a dead huntsman spider was being dragged along by what could only be described as, and please take a moment to imagine this, an insect of huge proportions looking like a cross between a prawn and a cockroach.

The spider was not a small one, it was at least the size of my face, but this spiny fellow was having no problems hauling it along towards his lair. Having become accustomed to meeting unusual creatures, I didn't panic, I merely retraced my steps backwards to keep a safe distance away.

As I started my retreat, the critter caught sight of me and got quite concerned that I was going to take his lunch away, and so decided to have a rather defensive dance with me.

I took a step away, it took one forward. I took a side step, and to my astonishment, so did he. At this point I was rather unnerved. Goose pimples had started to prick up all along my right side and up to my neck. Using my washing basket as cover, I ran like billy-o back into the sanctuary of the house, slamming the door shut behind me.

Through the bedroom window, I managed to take a couple of photographs of it, which I later used to back up my explanation of why Max's T-shirts were once again ruined. I then took time to research this fearless creature, and this is what I found out:

Spider wasps are generally found in the summer months and are a common sight in Australian backyards all over the country – even in Tasmania. They are from the family *Pompilidae* and are found in the order *Hymenoptera* – the same as ants and bees. The difference is that they are solitary and nest alone, not in a colony.

Although the one I found was orange, they can also be blue, grey and white, or just plain black. But even if they were a pretty pastel pink, a confrontation would still shock you.

They come in different sizes. The largest you would probably see is about 3.5cm, although I'm sure the one I saw (or should I say, the one that saw *me*) was much bigger. The female spider wasps look dangerous and have a powerful sting, but you will be pleased to know they are not aggressive towards people and can be safely ignored.

Spiders, on the other hand, better watch out: female spider wasps can be seen prowling around the garden searching under leaves and bark for a nice juicy huntsman or wolf spider, their wings flickering rapidly and bodies jerking about. Once she has found herself a suitable spider, she stings it to paralyse it, before dragging it back to her burrow in the ground where she will sit on it and lay an egg.

When the larva hatches, it starts to eat the spider, which may I add, is still alive. When mature enough, the larvae pupates to emerge as an adult the next summer.

Encounter 3 – Water Scorpion

A part of living in Australia that I appreciate almost every day is the glory of an early morning swim in the privacy of my own backyard. Most mornings I awake at 6.30 am and take half an hour to swim peacefully, breathing in the beauty I have around me and to feel grateful for all I have. After my swim I always feel relaxed and ready to take on whatever the day brings.

As soon as the children awake, I transform, and begin flying hither and thither to get everyone's lunchboxes/library bags/guitars and hockey sticks ready for school.

So my morning swim is really important to me, for my own sanity and for the safety of my children.

Imagine therefore my horror one morning when I found I had company in my pool. During the night a couple of leaves and, occasionally, some other foliage may drop into the water. I normally pick them out as I swim along, but this particular morning, as I was fully submerged and was returning to the surface with a rather large leaf I had retrieved from the bottom, I noticed a large black wiggling insect swimming frantically above where I was about to take my breath. I turned tail and swam to the other side of the pool, jumping out coughing and spluttering.

I located the fishing net and hunted down my uninvited swimming partner. On closer inspection I found it had a hideous pair of pincers at the front, a long spiky tail at the back and a rather unfriendly face. Needless to say, I found it a new home over the back of our fence – I hope it was very happy there.

Water scorpions are not attractive creatures. They resemble actual scorpions, with their front grasping legs, but these are just for show as they actually inflict their painful bite from the rostrum held under the head. Fortunately they tend not to terrorise humans and are quite happy to snack on mosquito wrigglers, tadpoles and small fish.

They have a rather unnerving respiratory siphon jutting out from the rear end. This is used to access air by resting the tip on the surface of the water. This siphon is very long and is responsible for half the scorpion's body length, which is generally about 6.5cm.

Scorpions are usually found in shallow, muddy water where they can hide away and wait patiently for their prey. Not therefore often found in swimming pools and I know of only one other family who has discovered one – so please don't worry too much!

Encounter 4 – Cane Toads

I love living in the sub-tropical climate of Queensland. I have become accustomed to the sudden downpours of torrential rain followed by vast, cloudless blue skies. I love the fact that the children walk home after school with their shoes in their bags so they can wade barefoot through the warm rainwater puddles. All this is glorious during the day, but if these downpours happen in the evening and you are in an area that is not very well lit, you may find yourself tripping over or squelching onto huge, slimy cane toads.

I have never been a fan of frogs of any size or shape, especially after a disturbing encounter in England when my cat brought one home through the cat flap. Once I had released the amphibian from the drooling jaws of my cat and got him suitably restrained, I tried to flick the little green bag of bones out of the front door with a dustpan. Unfortunately it didn't realise I was trying to free it and it ricocheted back towards me, catching one of its toes in my long curly hair, and began gyrating ferociously to escape.

My screams could probably have been misinterpreted as those of a murder victim as I shook my head from side to side to release its tangled grip. Eventually it plopped onto the floor and with a disgusted look, hopped quickly out of the door, still clutching some ginger strands of hair.

The cat was locked in the kitchen and the cat flap was taped up and never, ever used again.

Traumatised as I had been by this frog episode, I was utterly horrified when I was first confronted by a cane toad with its almighty, lumpy body and intimidating eyes. But like most phobias, once I faced it head on, I got used to seeing them about and I now have no irrational fear of one hitching a ride in my hair. I wouldn't be thrilled, mind, but I could cope.

Cane toads were brought to Australia in June 1935 from Hawaii in an effort to control the cane beetle, which causes havoc to the sugar cane crops. The adult beetles eat the leaves of the plants and the larvae hatch underground and eat the roots, so you can see why they thought importing something to eat them might be a good idea.

102 toads arrived, and settled happily into captivity and began to breed at an astonishing rate. By August 1935 more than 3,000 toads were released into North Queensland and more in other areas of the state. Due to environmental concerns, the releases were limited for a while until September 1936, when they were once again set free to roam the land.

It is now known that they have multiplied to over 200 million, blanketing their way across Queensland and over the border, to New South Wales in 1978 and the Northern Territory in 1984. It is estimated that these toads migrate at an average of 25 miles a year!

Research has discovered that the cane toads in the vanguard of their advance have evolved longer legs, larger bodies and faster movement, enabling them to travel farther. The downside for them is that 10% of these top toads have also developed arthritis.

They are now regarded as a feral species, in the same category as rabbits, foxes, cats and the Giant Mimosa (an invasive weed) and have been found to spread diseases affecting local biodiversity. So maybe it wasn't such a good idea after all.

Another interesting piece of trivia about cane toads is that they excrete a chemical called bufotenin, which under the Australian drug laws is a class 1 drug, the same classification as heroin and cocaine. But before you all rush out trying to find a toad to lick, you should be warned that they only excrete bufotenin in very small amounts and other toxins in relatively large doses, so toad licking could result in serious illness or death.

Encounter 5 – The Australian Cockroach

I used to go on a lot of camping holidays as a child with my parents and two sisters; we would load up the car to within an inch of its life and go abroad. So I had encountered many different insects, mainly in my sleeping bag, from an early age.

Cockroaches were always rife in the toilet blocks, but I would just avoid them and they would go on their merry way.

Arriving in Australia, I found myself once again confronted by a whopper of a cockroach in the bathroom. Feeling slightly nervous of its size I managed to coax it onto a dustpan and headed for the back door. Halfway there, its black shiny shell opened up, a pair of wings appeared and it took flight about head height and straight for me. My shrill screams of terror made Max come running from the lounge room, to find me shrunken on the floor with my T-shirt firmly over my head. This blighter was not going to get stuck in my hair.

Luckily these encounters soon stopped when we had the house treated by a pest controller, an invaluable service that all Australians have done regularly to avoid these blood-curdling moments.

Australian cockroaches are originally from Asia and have adapted to the household environment. They are scavengers and carry serious diseases such as salmonella, dysentery and other stomach complaint organisms. They feed on almost anything, and even the cleanest homes fall victim to these pests due to the minute food deposits that can get caught under refrigerators and dishwashers.

They are about 3.5cm long but their antennae (longer than their body) make them look longer still. They appear mostly at night, and have three sets of long spiny legs which enable them to run fast, allowing them to run rings around a sleepy human desperately trying to round one up with a dustpan and brush.

Of course the little blighters also have wings and although the sight of one heading for your face is shocking, they aren't famed for their flying expertise, preferring to dart about all over the floor. They can, however, squeeze their flat, broad bodies into ridiculously tight places, so if you do want to catch one, you have to be lightning fast before it bolts under the kitchen cupboard to rub its grubby little body in places you daren't imagine.

The Humble Magpie: a Warning

I wouldn't blame you for wondering what on earth a magpie could do that would be in any way dangerous. For most of the year they are not aggressive, but for four to six weeks, during the months of August to November, when they are nesting, these birds act as though they are demonically possessed as they defend their territory vigorously.

People walking past can well be seen as invaders, which prompts the birds to fly low and fast over them, clacking their bills as they go in a haunting fashion. Only if they feel extremely threatened, will they strike the intruder on the head with beak or claws. I expect that makes you feel much better.

Many people change their cycle routes and walking tracks during this season, to avoid being swooped on, as a magpie attack can be quite alarming, even for the onlookers.

Magpie Self-Defence Tips

Here are some rather bizarre methods to avoid falling victim to a frenzied attack:

- Magpies are less likely to swoop if you look at them. Try to keep an eye on the bird, at the same time edging carefully away. Alternatively, you could draw or sew on a pair of eyes to the back of a hat, and wear it when walking through the area. Maybe try wearing sunglasses on the back of your head.

- Wear a bicycle helmet or any sort of head protection. Even an ice-cream container will help.

- Carry an open umbrella, or a small branch above your head, but be careful not to swing it at the magpie as this will provoke an attack.

- If you are riding a bicycle when a magpie swoops, get off and wheel it quickly through the area.

- This may not be helpful, but if you see them swooping in the distance, turn around and find another route!

- Finally, try to avoid watching Alfred Hitchcock's *The Birds* during this season; it'll only make you paranoid.

It's only now, after I have done the research, that I could have warned my dear Welsh friend who took it as a personal attack when the magpies clipped her ears every morning on her way to school. I now know that wielding that enormous stick at them was probably not in her best interest.

Friends Found in the Home

Luckily there are some creatures that you may find in your house, which you *won't* feel a compulsion to either squish with a thong (flip-flop to you) or usher out the back door.

Geckoes are cute, fun and sometimes friendly, but more importantly they successfully rid the home of cockroaches, silverfish and spiders. Geckoes don't go out hunting for the sometimes huge cockroaches that find their way inside, but simply devour their young before they grow, multiply and reach plague proportions.

Some people swear by lizards, and often recommend keeping a breeding pair in your home. They will find their own little niche somewhere around. You don't have to feed or water them and children love to see them about the house, sometimes stuck to the ceiling defying gravity with their suction-like pads on their feet.

Of course, there are a couple of small downsides. At first, I used to shoo any geckoes out of the house, after finding a few left over tails behind curtains and under cabinets. I thought my cat had been snacking on the bodies and leaving the tails as trophies, but I now know that lizards shed their tails when frightened or cornered as a self-defence mechanism to bamboozle predators.

They also leave little droppings about the house when they scurry about during the night, but this is quickly remedied by a baby wipe which I find far less gross than bagging up a steaming dog turd in the park. They do also sometimes cluck, known scientifically as barking, which sounds strange and quite loud considering their tiny bodies. But I think you will agree that this is a small price to pay after you have encountered your first season of flying cockroaches.

TOP TIP

If you see an unusual creature, simply take its photo, download it and send it to this chap who will identify it for you for free. What an excellent resource!

www.whatsthatbug.com

Resources

Information on Visiting South Australia

www.southaustralia.com
www.topfoodandwinetours.com.au
www.tourkangarooisland.com.au

Australian Snakes and Spiders

www.whatsthatbug.com (free bug identification site)
www.usyd.edu.au/anaes/venom/snakebite.html
www.spiders.com.au (they even offer a free spider chart, handy for emergency identification purposes).

6: Home to Roost

We chose Queensland as our place to settle as we had already visited the state and found the climate to be most agreeable, with average temperatures between 10°C and 21°C in winter and 21°C and 29°C in the summer. Although humidity can be an issue, this can be tempered by the cooler sea breezes in coastal areas. The state has 300 days of sunshine a year and an economy that is beginning to boom as more and more people make the move up to the Sunshine State. Just what we were looking for in our Aussie adventure.

Brisbane Bound

We had researched where to stay in Brisbane before we had left England. The thought of staying in one motel room with children, although maybe a cheaper option, really didn't appeal to us. We stumbled upon an incredibly helpful couple, Rob and Lesley. Having themselves made the move to Australia with their children several years earlier, and after relocating *twice*, once from Perth, then from Melbourne, before eventually settling in Brisbane, they knew all to too well about the tribulations a short-term stay in a new country can bring.

So they set up a company to help us Brits have a slightly less worrying start to the experience of emigrating, by equipping us with all we need to know when first arriving in Oz. Not only are you armed with information at your finger tips and on the other end of the phone line, but they have a couple of wonderful houses on offer for you to rent for whatever timescale you feel is appropriate, subject to availability.

We chose a three bedroom, two bathroom town house in a relatively new complex with a community swimming pool in a suburb called Hendra, about 10 minutes from the airport and very near to all the areas we wanted to look at seriously.

The house we chose was practically brand new, with wonderful modern fixtures and fittings; three spacious bedrooms with built-in wardrobes. The master bedroom had a balcony, an en suite with a huge shower and a cavernous walk-in wardrobe. Downstairs, the well-equipped kitchen/diner/lounge room opened out to an outside eating area where you could unwind after a day of searching for your future piece of Australian life. This all appears after you have parked your car in the remote-controlled double garage and ambled past another downstairs cloakroom. A great start!

The search was on. There were many suburbs of Brisbane we wanted to check out, all for different reasons.

Some were new areas, where they had developed new communities, with their own schools, shopping centres and resources, all sensibly built in beautiful leafy surroundings with bike paths and walkways. Spacious family homes with privacy in mind, unlike in Essex, where even in the most exclusive of developments, you could smell the sweet fragrance of your next-door neighbours' washing. And unless you were the owner of a Smart car, getting out of your vehicle in the garage was a feat only contortionists could confidently conquer.

So every day we would pack up a large hamper of delicious picnic food and stick a pin in the map to choose the destination of the day. And every day we would come home weary and confused as to where to set up home.

All these places seemed so very attractive. Anywhere that

has the benefit of the sun most of the year looks infinitely better than somewhere doused in grey skies. But there was just something missing that I couldn't quite put my finger on.

As we had made such a huge decision to emigrate, we wanted to get it right first time, and for me, that meant living near one of the glorious Queensland beaches. For some reason I assumed that Brisbane had beaches, but this doesn't appear to be the case.

It claims to have beaches, with places encouragingly named Nudgee Beach for example, but unfortunately I found Nudgee Beach to have an eerie, desolate feel, occupied mainly by peculiar-looking fishermen standing alone along the edge of mud-flats. I felt just like I was standing on the beach at Southend-on-Sea, looking across the Thames Estuary, only feeling hotter and more disturbed.

Even the promising Redland Bay area was a forlorn expanse of muddy vastness.

The only token piece of beach is, although spectacular, a man-made sandy swimming area in a place called Southbank, right in the heart of the city. Hats off to them for putting a little segment of tranquillity amongst the hustle and bustle of the city, but if you ever decide to go there on a Sunday afternoon for a family outing, expecting a pleasurable swim and the making of sandcastles, you will quickly be faced with a different picture.

Hoards of crowds, all desperately try to secure their own four square feet's worth of sand, by spreading out a couple of oversized beach towels and screwing in vibrantly coloured sun parasols. It was too similar to an unseasonable day at any of the British seaside towns, minus the kiss-me-quick hats, novelty lollipops and the overpowering aroma of fish and chips and, on occasion, urine.

Our search started to take us further afield. We tried Redcliffe, which was very pleasant, but had quite an old-fashioned feeling – slightly too many retirement homes, and names like Brighton, Margate and Scarborough, which I didn't feel would have the right type of vibe for my Australian address.

So we carried on slightly north, towards the Sunshine Coast. I had secretly always wanted to live there as it just looked idyllic, with glorious beaches and tropical rainforests. I didn't really think it was somewhere people actually would live though, as it seemed more like a holiday destination, and I feared there would be a lack of infrastructure and, being an hour away from Brisbane, a lack of work opportunities.

But I had been thumbing through the guest book at the Hendra house and had found a family that had made the move up there. I contacted them for more information, and it was there we were headed.

Imagine for a moment, the kids are bickering in the back of the car, time is running out on the short-term lease, your cats are due out of quarantine any day and a container-load of furniture is about to arrive. You start reconsidering areas you had initially ruled out just because of the anxiety building up inside.

You have put so much into this venture and you've started to get pretty despondent about the whole immigration process. It seems you will never find that dream place you were looking for…

…and then, suddenly, you step out from the confines of

the car and are met with magnificent Norfolk pine trees, surrounding a glorious honey-coloured bay, the sky and sea so sublimely blue they virtually merge into one, and warm sea breezes gently caressing your skin while rainbow lorikeets bursting with unimaginable colour chirp merrily overhead. On the beach families laugh and frolic, looking like they have been precisely positioned for an advertisement for 'living the dream'.

This was IT.

Before we all got too excited, we knew that it wouldn't work if the place was devoid of shops, schools and general day-to-day amenities. On our journey up, although the Bruce Highway is the main route, we had encountered a whole lot of forest and nothingness, but with our new-found enthusiasm, we set off to explore further.

We met up with the family I had contacted through the Hendra guest book and they proved to be delightfully welcoming. They told us their story of how they had come to find this area, how the job situation was going, also all about the local schools and community. We had told them of our concerns about being so far out of Brisbane and maybe feeling out in the sticks, which they understood, especially as they had lived in the south of England also, and knew only too well about living somewhere so over-populated.

But Brisbane was only an hour away; it often took double that to travel to London from where we lived in Essex, 40 miles away, due to the horrendous delays on the roads and, often, the old leaves on the railway lines.

So once our new friends had inundated us with information about hospitals, schools and everything else imaginable, we decided we weren't out in the sticks any longer. This was to be our new home.

The next week or so was spent zooming up and down the Bruce Highway, having interviews with my son's new school, buying uniforms and amongst many other pressing matters, finding a house to rent in the school zone.

After combing through the choices on offer, we eventually narrowed ours down to three houses (we were limited in our choice as many landlords do not allow animals). After seeing two rather uninviting houses, we started to consider other options for our cats... like euthanasia.

But luckily – for them – the final house we looked at had everything we wanted on our list. Four bedrooms, a large lounge room, air conditioning for those stifling summer months which lay ahead, a wonderful elevated view from the big backyard and of course an enormous sparkling swimming pool.

The house itself was in a slight state of disrepair. The bathrooms had seen better days and the kitchen was probably extremely modern in the early 80s, but over time, had developed a rusty electric four-ring hob and had a dreadful wooden-edged worktop, which looked as though it harboured other people's undesirable germs.

The carpets were almost threadbare and had many questionable stains on them, but, we thought, nothing a few huge rugs and a bottle of carpet cleaner couldn't fix. And after all, we needed somewhere to live – and fast. Once our furniture was in, we could live with the not-so-modern facilities.

So after mounds of paperwork and point scoring we were accepted as tenants and signed up for the next six months. This was a huge relief, as our shipment was arriving the following week and the cats were flying up from the airport quarantine in Melbourne to Brisbane in a matter of days.

We moved in on June 30 and our shipment arrived the next morning.

The removal men were very organised and had a checklist so that we could tick off all the boxes that the UK firm had printed out. It felt like Christmas as we unwrapped all our homely wares; not one item was chipped or broken, (my sister hadn't helped with this packing) we were highly impressed, and couldn't thank the removal men enough, who replied, "Too easy": a phrase I would encounter many, many more times in my life in Queensland.

Renting Rules

As I mentioned earlier, when we first arrived in Queensland we had already pre-booked our short-term accommodation with a small company called Brisbane Bound, who were an invaluable first step in emigrating.

The owner, Rob, was only too happy to give us a reference, enabling us to meet the strict guidelines to be able to rent our first house. Obviously, we were model tenants, so he didn't mind...

I doubt he would be so accommodating if we had trashed the joint and stolen the toaster.

Back in England, I used to surf the internet for available properties in our price range; so when we arrived in Australia – laptop in hand – we looked up properties in the area we were going to concentrate on. We thought we'd be fully armed and ready to pounce after having viewed those images online.

Unfortunately, when it comes to visiting the properties, you often find many other families lined up to do the same. It is normal practice in Australia for rental properties to be viewed at an appointed time and some house inspections gather crowds of prospective tenants, which is quite intimidating – especially when you find somewhere you really like.

Renting Requirements

It is best to go fully prepared, so here is a list of real estate agent requirements:

Proof of Identification (minimum of 100 points)

Type of Proof	Points
Last four rent receipts, tenant ledger or rates notice (if owned)	50
Driver's licence, 18+ card or passport	40
Photo ID	30
Minimum of two references from previous landlord/agent	20
Current motor vehicle registration papers	10
Copy of previous Telstra (telephone), Energex or mobile phone statement	10
Pay slip, Centrelink income and assets statement	10
Bank statement, group certificate, letter from sccountant (if self-employed)	10
Copy of birth certificate	10
Pension or health-care card (not Medicare)	10

> ## TOP TIP
>
> If you are straight off the boat, so to speak, you won't have a lot of these documents yet. You can use a UK driver's licence and passport for photo ID. Any other ID you may have access to is useful, such as an offer of employment letter. Bank statements can also be used.

Proof of Income

If no employment has been arranged yet, a bank statement in most cases is acceptable. Generally the requirement for rent payment is 30% of weekly income as rent (similar to bank consideration). There is no fixed amount required in your bank account but it would need to show that, if you are unable to find employment for a considerable time, you can nevertheless afford to pay the rent.

Rental References

Basically a rental reference is used to prove that a prospective tenant will take care of the property. If you have recently sold a property or are letting your own home in the UK, then a written reference from your agents would be helpful.

In this case, a personal referee can become very important. If you have someone in Australia who can be used as a personal referee that would help. If the only contacts you have are in the UK then email addresses are better than phone numbers due to time differences and cost. Also, if you are using a relocation company, this can be used to qualify prospective tenants.

If Your Application Is Accepted

Before you move into the property six weeks rent in advance will be required, made up as follows:

- Equivalent of four weeks' rent for bond (deposit)
- Equivalent of two weeks' rent in advance

Most offices do not accept bond transfers (a deposit transferred from the rental property you are leaving) under any circumstances.

Of course individual agencies have their own requirements and prospective tenants must ensure they adhere to these.

Fingers Crossed

Once you have filled it in, take your application back to the agent, who will then submit it to the landlord. Then you just have to wait for it to be processed, which can take up to a week. You will be informed as soon as a decision has been made.

TOP TIP

When you first move into your rental property, it is important to note down all the marks that are there, and any other broken tiles on floors or bathroom walls; holes in the fly screens, dusty ceiling fans and obvious marks on the carpets, walls or ceilings. The rental agent should have made a list of all these items, but to be on the safe side you should double-check the list before you move in, in case there are any discrepancies when you leave and want to get your bond back.

Make sure you agree who is going to pay (ie you or the landlord) for garden care and pool maintenance; this will also be written in the tenancy agreement.

It is not unusual for the landlord to pay for a pool maintenance company to visit once a month, and the tenant to pay for the chemicals, so that is something to be aware of.

We have always paid for our own gardener to visit once every few weeks to cut lawns and take the dead fronds (huge palm tree leaves) to the tip. This saves so much time and during the hot summer months I can think of nothing worse than being covered in grass clippings, then having to trundle sweatily down to the tip.

When you get into your rental property, you will be visited every three months by a house inspector. A letter from your agent will tell you the date they will be arriving, and you can decide to be there whilst they inspect or they can let themselves in. You can let them know if you have any minor problems with the property, but major problems are best communicated direct to the rental management agent – who will probably want the problem in an email as well – and then the matter should be dealt with fairly quickly.

TOP TIP
If you do decide to rent when you first arrive, although you won't have to think about paying water rates, it is still a smart idea to think ahead when you are buying your new appliances and choose ones with a good water conservation rating. Being water conscious is a good habit to get into!

The good thing about renting (once you have finally managed to secure a house) is that you pay for gas, electricity and phone bills but not rates, as the landlord is responsible for them. In some areas, mainline gas is not available, but you can still have it supplied to your home, as there are many professional companies that deliver gas bottles. So you will still be cooking with gas!

Water Restrictions

I was entertaining the children one afternoon in a local park when we had first arrived in Brisbane, when I noticed one of the many bubblers (drinking water fountains) had become stuck somehow and was leaking. As I went over, thinking I should do a good deed and try and fix it, a woman walking past the park shouted over to me, "Oi, are you gonna fix that?"

I politely replied, in an apologetic English manner, and explained that I was in fact attempting to as it had become stuck. She steamed over to where I was fiddling and gave it a few bashes and somehow managed to stop the flow. She then turned tail and muttered, "I'll have to get onto them about that" and waddled away.

The conservation of water has become an important issue in Australia.

Although Australia has its fair share of torrential downpours and floods, the dams in some states may still be under capacity, which means stringent water restrictions can be in place. It is frowned upon if you water the garden, or wash your car with a hose if there is a ban, so it is advisable to check with your area to see what your local water restriction level is before you decide to put the sprinkler on or top up the pool.

There are several levels of water restriction, number one being the least restrictive, going up to level eight. Try adhere to the rules to avoid being verbally abused: most Australians are passionate about water conservation!

Vacating Your Rental Property

When the time comes to *leave* your rental property, there are more rules that you must abide by. Firstly if you have had a pet (dog/cat/kangaroo) living at the property, you are required to get a pest control company in to fumigate the house. The same goes for carpet cleaning: there are dozens of companies listed in the yellow pages or online and all in the same price range.

TOP TIP
To save time, check for a sticker on the inside of one of the kitchen cupboards – usually the one under the sink.
Normally the last company that has cleaned the carpets or performed pest control leaves one stuck there.

If you decide to vacate the property *before* the end of your lease, you are liable to pay the rent up until the time you were contracted to leave. You should give your agent/landlord plenty of notice, approximately 21 days. Fortunately in most cases you can usually find someone who will take over the lease so you can then have your bond returned.

I would highly recommend renting for at least the first six months, because even if you are familiar with an area, you always find out more when you are actually living there. I know plenty of Brits who jumped straight in and bought a property as soon as they landed, using the old "why should we be paying off someone else's mortgage?" chestnut — only to discover that they weren't as keen on the area or the house as they had though and decided to move again. So take heed, rent first, get to grips with the Aussie way of life and take things sl-o-o-o-w-l-y!

Real Estate and Renting Jargon Translated

Here are some words, abbreviations and phrases that you will come across and their UK equivalent:

Lowset: a bungalow. Bungalow is not a term used here, apart from when referring to a 'gentleman's bungalow', which is a huge rambling property made of brick.

Highset: a property that has been built on poles or stilts (apparently to capture the breezes – most common in Queensland when referred to as a *Queenslander*).

Two level or double storey: a normal house, just like in the UK, with an upstairs.

Character home: older style home.

Inground pool: this simply means that the property has a swimming pool. An 'above ground pool' means it is more of a temporary type, and sits on top of the ground.

Saltwater inground pool: real estate agent jargon to make the swimming pool sound more attractive – when in fact *all* pools are mainly salt water and they *all* have added chemicals – or we'd all end up with stagnant water-borne ailments!

Wet edge pool: an infinity pool – one that has the illusion of water running off the edge.

Robe, BIR, or walk-in robe: a built-in wardrobe – a *walk-in* is a big one, usually in the master bedroom.

DLUG and SLUG: double or single lock-up garage. The lock-up means the garage door will lock behind you, which is excellent if you have a remote control fitted: simply drive off and press a button.

Weatherboard: a wooden house.

Carport: occasionally the property may have had the garage converted into another room. The car will be in a carport, which they will have fitted, or there may even be a simple canvas sail hung over the drive.

Undercover deck: outdoor entertaining area, in the shade.

Yard: garden.

Fully screened: all opening windows and doors will have fly screens.

Fully ducted A/C or reverse cycle A/C: *reverse cycle* means the air conditioning unit can both cool down and heat up your home. *Fully ducted* means that each room in the house will have an air-conditioned outlet (very posh!).

Rumpus room: family room.

Laundry: utility room – a separate room for your washing machine, tumble dryer and ironing board etc. Will also have a huge butler-style sink which is extremely handy.

Gourmet kitchen: top of the range kitchen units and appliances.

Kleenmaid appliances: high quality kitchen appliances.

Homebuying Basics
A Look Back in Time

When you are completely confident with your new-found area, it is inevitable that you will want to buy your first home, and start setting down your roots.

The experience of buying your Aussie home should feel like a walk in the park in comparison to your UK experience, which probably felt more like a walk through a minefield, in the fog.

How can this be possible?

Because of a chap by the name of Robert Torrens who came to Australia in the early colonial days. Around the year 1858 he thought up a brilliant idea for simplifying the complex legal process of selling houses. He based his system on the method of registering ownership of ships according to merchant shipping law. At a sweep he did away with the complex old English land laws which had their basis in medieval times.

It boils down to this simple fact: when the owners sell their house the *Certificate of Title* is known as *Good Title* and guaranteed in law. This eliminates the need to constantly check back into the depths of the past to every owner that has ever lived there, just to make sure the property was theirs in the first place!

It's used in Australia and in several other countries, in fact the *Torrens Title* is a great legal export but has never caught on in Britain, where an astonishing one house sale in every three, fails.

The *Torrens Title* is the most common for standard residential suburban homes – but there are other titles too, depending on the type of property. For more information on title deeds, contact the land titles office in your state or territory.

Before We Start...

There are some expressions and phrases you will be glad to know, are simply unheard of in Australia, for instance:

1. In a chain...
The situation just never arises. Why? Because you can actually nominate the exact date which is mutually agreeable to you and the sellers (vendors) for the big

move, knowing with every confidence that it will happen on that date. If you are in a line of people each wishing to buy the next person's property, but each needing the proceeds of their own house sale to do so, it is quite simple.

The real estate agents will talk together to make sure everyone has the same date for completion, (known as *settlement* in Oz), and so it happens in the most orderly and civilized fashion. The first settlement takes place, the proceeds are moved on to purchase the next property and so on down the line without a hair out of place. There are no nail-biting moments, or nightmares that someone might fail at the last moment – because everyone can rely on the security of the contract.

2. Gazumping
This is strictly not allowed by law. You pay the exact price agreed in the contract, not a cent more or a cent less. Once again you can rely absolutely on the contract.

3. Exchange Contracts
Clearly this is another leftover from the Medieval English land laws. No doubt this had a great deal of importance when buying your average size castle, complete with moat that you wanted to protect the king – but it is of doubtful use here. The position in Oz is – you want the house, agree the price and arrange a date for settlement. You may have put some conditions in the contract. Check it all over carefully and sign. That's it. No more mucking around, you have yourself a house!

TOP TIP
House sizes are measured (and referred to)
in square metres (or simply squares).
So, one square metre = 10.76 square feet

Here are some pointers to get you started.

Open for Viewing

Searching for your dream home will be much the same as the UK, checking out the property section of the newspapers or surfing the internet. Oddly enough, people don't make a beeline for the real estate office as much as they do in the UK.

When you have found one or more properties that you like the sound of (or the price of), it's time to go and view them. In the advertisement you will see the words *Open*, *Open House* or *Open Inspection*. This is a general invitation to prospective buyers to give the house a once-over at a strictly set time, lasting 30 minutes to an hour. The weekend is the favourite time for viewing and sometimes they invite twilight viewings, which sound pretty, but of course, this will also make the house look prettier too.

The *open* will be conducted by the real estate agent; you will not see the owners so you can look around carefully and ask questions without any feeling of embarrassment.

This is of a great relief to me, as when I was selling my house in England, I was absolutely terrible at showing people round my own house. I watched all the TV programmes on how to sell my property. I did exactly what Sarah Beeny told me to do, so I thought I would easily coax a prospective buyer into biting my arm off to get into my house.

Once again, this wasn't to be the case. I think the desperation of wanting to get to Australia as soon as I could, made any attempts at looking sane dissipate. Although the couples who traipsed through our house were probably quite keen, all manner of interest quickly waned once I had bored them with every conceivable nook and cranny. How could they *not* want to know about the baked bean-tin carousel in the top left-hand kitchen cupboard?

Once, I accompanied a gentleman upstairs, eager to show off our magnificently boarded-out loft, complete with easy-up ladder. I couldn't understand why he would not want to even poke his head up through the hatch, I mean — even out of politeness I would do it and surely all men love a loft? How was I to know he had a prosthetic leg?

Can you empathise with my relief for never having to conduct another viewing?

So go to lots of *opens* and get the feel for what is available. Don't be afraid to talk to the real estate agent. This person is a professional who has invested a lot of money and time into getting the required qualifications. They want a lot of happy clients, that's you, so that their business grows. It is in their interest to help you.

Time to Make 'em an Offer!

The agent will write the offer up for you. If you need a mortgage it will read, "subject to loan approval" (up to a certain interest percentage). You are able to make the offer conditional, on factors such as a satisfactory inspection or valuation report. If the sellers are then happy with the offer, they will countersign it, at which point the contract becomes legally binding on both parties. You do get a short cooling down period (which varies from state to state, but is generally from three to ten working days). If you do change your mind within this time, it must be done in writing.

If however, you had laid down some conditions and they have not been met, you can still withdraw beyond this period.

If all is well, a deposit is required and this will go into the real estate agent's trust account. (This of course will come off the purchase price.) Within days a mortgage valuer will be out to check the property. If the lender is satisfied it fulfils the terms of the contract you have a done deal. Congratulations!

Please note however, that this is just a general outline. It varies a little from state to state. In South Australia for example the real estate agent is trained to write up a legal contract for both parties, no solicitor is required and it works very well. Other states will require a solicitor; however the speed and efficiency of the system will astonish and delight you.

TOP TIP

Make sure you have the house insured immediately in your name. It is now your responsibility, so if it burns to the ground, you will have a mortgage to pay on a heap of embers sitting on a block of land.

Under the Hammer

You will find many homes on the auction market. Although this doesn't mean that the property *has* to go to auction. If the right offer is made beforehand, the owners are often happy to forgo the entire auction circus.

However owners may well insist on selling under auction terms. This means no cooling off period as is usually the case at an auction.

To purchase at auction you must have all your finances in place, plus you must have 10% of the purchase price ready for immediate deposit. If you are successful at the fall of the hammer you have an insurable interest in the property. This means if the house burns down the sale still goes ahead because what you purchase is 'the whole of the land', so again, it is in your best interest to insure the bricks and mortar.

In Australia auctions are a popular way of selling luxury homes or homes that are unique and difficult to price accurately. Often a real estate agent or even an owner will want to sell by auction to establish the true market price of the home. Often deceaseds' estates, or bank repossessions are sold in this manner as it is a transparent way to gain the true market price for a property. Auctions do not mean, as sometimes in Britain, that a broken down property is being offered for sale – far from it. Auctions are also favoured because the sale will happen within a structured time frame.

Auctions are sometimes held on site (at the property) or, as is becoming popular in some areas, in an auction room.

If you want to bid at auction, talk to the real estate agent, they have seen it all before and will give you expert advice. The main thing is to stick to your budget. The agent will be able to give you a ballpark figure as to the expected final selling price, but it is only an estimate. The owner will have placed a reserve price on the property; this has to be done because otherwise in theory, the property could be knocked down to a very low bid. This reserve price is a secret between the owner and the auctioneer. If the bidding is slow the auctioneer may pause the auction and go into a discussion with the owner. This is not sinister; this is a realistic discussion to possibly adjust the reserve price. The property may not be sold below the reserve.

ODD SPOT

When you have signed your contract, its best if you don't do the British thing and carry on looking at other houses. If by chance you find something even dreamier than your dream house, you can't do anything about it! Remember both you and your seller have a contract and that is why it runs so smoothly.

Homebuying Monetary Musts

Just as in the UK, lenders like to see that you are credit worthy, and that financially you are a good risk, but as you will have little or no credit history in Australia, it would be a great idea to take evidence of any mortgage arrangements you had in the UK.

I couldn't think of anything drearier for you than reading an entire chapter on acquiring a mortgage. Luckily I am not qualified to bore you with facts and figures, and there are dozens of mortgage brokers out there to assist you with making the right choice, so I'll pass the buck to them – and you can find 'them' in the resource section.

But, there are a couple of pieces of information, which I think are simply golden, so I will instead share those with you.

First Home Owner Grant (FHOG)

If you are a first-home buyer, you may be entitled to a first-time homebuyer grant. Some conditions do apply, but these conditions are not means tested and not restricted to the price of the property. The grant came into effect on 1 July 2000; it is an on-going scheme with no specified end date.

Stamping Out the Duty

Unfortunately, you cannot escape having to pay tax on your purchase price. Stamp duty varies, not only on the house price, but each state levies it at differing rates.

The good news is though, if you are a first-time buyer, in *some* states, there is no stamp duty to pay, providing the purchase price is under $500,000. So go on, make 'em an offer they can't refuse!

Resources

Renting

www.brisbanebound.com
www.realestate.com.au
www.domain.com.au
www.open2view.com.au
www.rent-a-home.com.au (for short-term accommodation, holiday rentals or corporate accommodation)

For more information on rental bonds phone freecall 1800 422 621 (in Australia)

Buying

www.reia.com.au (the real estate institute of Australia)
www.firsthome.gov.au (FHOG details)

Some big mortgage companies:
www.choicehomeloans.com.au
www.rams.com.au
www.onedirect.com.au
www.mortgagebrokerdirect.com.au

7: Shop 'til You Flop

The first time I went out to the supermarket I thought nothing of it, having done this arduous chore for many years. Unfortunately, I found the whole experience to be a feat in itself. At first, all appears normal. You get your trolley, walk in through the doors and are confronted with a fruit and veg section, just like any supermarket in Britain.

Too easy.

You are then challenged with familiar produce, only with unusual names. Examples are listed in the translation page.

To get you in the swing, one product worth its own mention, which I came across while looking for some WD40 for an irritating squeak emanating from my clutch pedal, was an Australian version entitled Start ya Bastard.

I also want to point out that unless you intend to spend weeks trying out new jars of mayonnaise in the desperate hope that you will find one that isn't in fact salad cream, head for S & W whole egg mayonnaise – it's just like Hellmann's, so you'll feel right at home. This has to be among my most favourite tips, as have you ever tried tuna mayonnaise sandwiches made with salad cream? It made me physically contort.

Another point worth mentioning is that it is impossible to buy Heinz spaghetti without some cheese content. All varieties have cheese, but most popular is the extra cheese. How horrid if you just want plain old tomato sauce. But it isn't bad enough to make you want to go back to England. Plus there are shops where you can purchase all your old Great British favourites, at extortionate prices.

After an hour and a half of wondering up and down aisles, examining every item as though it came from another solar system, then placing it in the trolley with a hopeful grunt and a shrug, I came to the end of the shop. Feeling a little confused, I retraced my steps until I came back to the entrance. No, I wasn't imagining it; there was actually no alcohol aisle. After further enquiries, it turns out you can't buy booze at a supermarket in some states in Australia; you have to go to a 'bottle shop'.

Having said that, when you start searching for said bottle shop, you then realise that there is one on every corner of every street, in varying sizes from your small run-of-the-mill off licence to the spectacular drive-through type, where you don't even have to get out of your car if you know what you want. Simply pop your boot and pay the guy… Now that's convenience.

So back in the supermarket, I was all done and ready to pay for my bizarre trolleyful. Having greeted the cashier (who seems genuinely happy to serve you) with the usual, "How you garrrn?", I started to load the conveyor belt, hoping I would be able to get to the other side to pack before every item had been bleeped, leaving me with a mound of dented bread and bruised bananas to cram into dozens of plastic bags which have no easy way of opening unless you have sweaty hands – a custom we British have become extremely accustomed to.

So imagine my astonishment when, as I raced to the end of the conveyor belt, my goods had been packed. Splendidly. The happy cashier not only acknowledged me and politely conversed, but also packed my bags for me.

I have to say, I felt a little uncomfortable with this level of hospitality on the first few occasions, and found myself trying to look busy, maybe pretending to be searching for something in my bag, or checking my mobile phone for messages, anything rather than look like a spare part on the other side of the till.

Now, I must warn you of the next obstacle. If you pay by cash, there is a process called rounding. You may remember this from your school days. In Oz they round cents up or down to the nearest five. This is because, in 1991, the one and two cent coins were discontinued and withdrawn from circulation. For instance, if your bill comes in at $153.97, you would actually be charged $154.00. The same goes the other way, if your shopping was $153.22, it would be $153.20. Quite easy, but if like me, you don't know about this unwritten rule and you rummage incessantly into the corners of your wallet, searching for the correct coinage by way of one and two cent coins, you do feel a bit of an idiot.

On the other hand, you could be paying with a credit card – couldn't be easier you think? Think again. Normally you would swipe your card, pop in a pin number and Bob's your Uncle. Oh no. This usually straightforward procedure becomes riddled with confusion,

"Will you be paying by cash or Eftpos?" the cashier will ask.

Eftpos? Eftpos? your mind races to make some kind of connection.

Well, let me tell you this rather horrid title stands for Electronic Fund Transfer at Point of Sale – whoever thought that Eftpos would make a catchy name is obviously quite insane.

Unfortunately, it doesn't end there, you will then get a list of options to choose from, which you must get right or face further humiliation.

"Cheque, savings or credit?" will be the next question.

Make sure you know which account you have your card linked to. It will be either one of those three and you must remember which one you applied for. If you don't, you face further embarrassment when the little screen on the swipe box reads: DECLINED.

Once you have chosen your correct account, or panicked and decided to pay in cash, you are now safe to exit the building, but I think now would be a perfectly appropriate time to try that drive-through bottle shop.

Let's Talk Shop

There are further shopping phrases, after you have recovered from the supermarket, that you may find confusing on your first visit to the mall. First they have *lay-by* which is when you wish to purchase an item, but you do not wish to pay for it on that day. Simply do your shopping, then instead of taking it to the checkout, make your way to the *lay-by* counter, where a helpful staff member will put your chosen items away for you through a back door (where they go then, no-one knows). Then they will arrange some type of fortnightly payment for you. You may think this is a bit of a palaver, but as the kids break up for their Christmas holidays so early, and for so long (six weeks) *and* because everyone goes to the wonderful refreshing mall with its air-conditioned comfort during December, it's a great idea to get all your shopping done as early as possible. And this comes from someone who normally does all of her shopping on Christmas Eve.

ODD SPOT

There are many shops with 'mart' in the title. There is Super A-Mart (furniture store); A-Mart All Sports (sports goods); K-Mart (reasonably priced variety store); and finally we have Bob Jane T-Mart (motor-vehicle tyre store)

Rain check means that you can put an item on *lay-by* when it's gone on offer, or *special*, as it's known here (which happens regularly). For instance, you see a new bicycle in one of the many special offer catalogues that are posted in your mailbox, and you pop down to K-Mart to get it. Of course by the time you get there, there are none left, but as long as the catalogue doesn't state "sorry, no rainchecks" you will be able to go to the *lay-by* counter and order that bicycle at the advertised price, and they will simply phone you when it's in stock.

The last phrase is *fly-buys*. Now this is literally just a reward points card with which you can earn yourself some goodies if you swipe it when you shop in certain stores. It's a bit like a nectar card in the UK, but I thought I would mention it, as I was terribly confused by

---

TOP TIP

Woolworth's here isn't like the former UK store, it's just a supermarket. In some states it is called Safeway. Big W is more like the British Woolworth's. They sell all sorts of stuff from CDs to tumble dryers, toys and bicycles and clothes. You can get some great bargains there.

---

the question: "Do you have fly-buys?"

I'm sure if it had been phrased, "Do you collect fly-buy points?" I would not, once again, have resembled a half-wit.

Once, when we had first arrived and we were shopping for bedroom furniture, we had just picked out the items we needed when the shop assistant floored us with a question: "So now you have all your beds on order, do you want to look at Manchester?"

She asked me again after my attempt at speech had failed. Why would I want to look at Manchester, I've just immigrated to Australia? I had no reason to go to the north of England, especially as I'd just bought four new beds. Why is this lady asking such a bizarre question?

My vacant expression allowed her plenty of time to explain that *Manchester* is actually a collective name for bed linen, towels and quilts (aka Doonas – don't ask). I later researched this peculiar expression, which led me to find that Australia used to import cotton from Manchester as it was the world's first industrialised city and dominant international centre of textile manufacture and cotton-spinning. All very commendable but how strange that nobody is aware of that term in England? Curiouser and curiouser, I thought.

Where's the VAT?

In Australia there is no such thing as VAT! There is however, GST...

GST (Goods and Services Tax) is levied on the supply of goods, services and other items at the rate of 10% on items sold or consumed in Australia.

It first took effect in July 2000, under the Federal Government and it replaced *WST (Wholesale Sales Tax)*.

The idea of this new system was to broaden the tax base and end the unfair tax advantage that businesses providing services had over businesses supplying goods. This was because since the *WST* was imposed in the 1930s, Australia's economy had evolved from being mainly goods-dominated to becoming more service-based.

Like VAT, *GST* is automatically taken into account on your shopping, so you need not worry about having to add it on yourself before you pay at the cash register.

There are some *GST* exempt items, such as:

- Basic food for human consumption
- Certain medical aids and appliances
- Other health services
- Cars for use by disabled people.

Here is a website for you to investigate further:
www.gstaustralia.com.au/

Clothing Sizes

Adults' clothes sizes are the same as the UK, which means they vary greatly from brand to brand, so it's trial and error again.

While I was out searching for baby clothes, which I had always thought I knew backwards, I was having great difficulty understanding what age was what.

TOP TIP
Children's clothes sizes often go up in age numbers and some brands only use even numbers so don't waste too much time searching for your child's exact age number. If you haven't seen any odd-number sizes, just grab an appropriate size and keep your receipt.

I gave up and quizzed my friends about why I was unable to find newborn sizes. The reason is that they tend to size their clothes using a number of zeros.

So here are the sizes in plain English. I have converted the kilos to pounds (approximately), just to help you out but Australia is totally metric, so you'll end up having to get into it!

Baby Clothing Sizes

Size Code	Plain English
00000	Premature baby 'Premy' (< 3kg or 6lb)
0000	Newborn (up to 4kg or 8lbs)
000	3 months (4–6kg or 8–13lbs)
00	6 months (6–8kg or 13–17lbs)
0	9 months (8–10kg or 17–22lbs)
1	12 months (10–11kg or 22–24lbs)
2	18 months (11–12kg or 24–26lbs)
2*	24 months (12–14kg or 24–30lbs)

* Note: 2 is used for both 18 and 24 months

Child Shoe Sizes

Children's shoe sizes are the same as the UK, until they get to the age of 12–18 months, when it changes to:

Age	UK	Australia
12–18 months	4	4–5
18–24 months	5	6
3 years	6	7
4 years	7	8
5 years	8	9
6 years	9	10
7 years	10	11
8 years	11	12
9 years	12	13

Adult Shoe Sizes (Women Only)

As long as I can remember, I have always bought an average size 5 shoe except occasionally when I may have had to try on a pair of 6s if I hadn't cut my toenails for a while. But I was horrified to find that I could no longer squeeze even my left pinkie into a pair of 5s here. Humidity does make you swell up a bit, but after trying on a 6, then a 7, I finally found myself the rather embarrassed owner of a pair of 8s. The term "sasquatch" sprang to mind.

Here are some more size conversions to help you discover the painful truth. Incidentally, it is only women's sizes that differ; men's are the same in both countries.

UK	4	5	6	7	8	9	10	11	12
Australia	6	7	8	9	10	11	12	13	14

Bra Sizes

Cup sizes are the same size in both countries, but the band sizing is completely different:

UK	32	34	36	38	40
Australia	10	12	14	16	18

Food Translation

Australian	English
Ice block/icy pole	Ice lolly
Lollies	Sweets
Chips	Crisps
Hot chips	Chips
Cheerios	Little Sausages
Snags	Sausages
Sanger	Sandwich
Chiko Roll (brand name)	Type of savoury snack
Avos	Avocados
Capsicum	Pepper
Zucchini	Courgette
Mandies	Mandarins
Bottle shop/bottle-o	Off Licence
Chook	Chicken
Esky (eskimo box)	Cool box
Champagne	Sparkling wine of *any* description!
Cask	Box of wine
Amber	Beer
Stubby	Bottle of beer
Tinny *	Can of beer
Slab	24 cans of shrink-wrapped beer

* Incidentally a tinny is a kind of small fishing boat, as well as a can of beer.

Homewares Translation

Australian	English
Manchester	Bed linen/towels etc
Doona	Continental quilt
Whipper snipper	Strimmer
Light globes	Light bulbs
Hill's hoist (brand name)	Rotary washing line
Glad wrap	Cling film
Vacuum cleaner	Hoover*

* Okay, so Brits say vacuum cleaner too but nobody calls them Hoovers in Oz

Clothes Translation

Australian	English
Joggers	Trainers (sports shoes)
Singlet	Vest
Shirt (plural is often Tees)	T-Shirt
Jocks	Men's underpants
Swimmers, bathers, togs, cozzie	Swimming costume
Thongs*	Flip-flops

* The ultimate in all embarrassing mistakes is the infamous thongs (insert your own joke here!)

8: School Daze

So we finally had a house, which we had double-checked was in the correct catchment for the highly recommended school. And as my son's first day came ever closer, I felt so nervous for him that the thought of it made my stomach knot up. This was the moment I had been dreading the most, waking up in a cold sweat in the middle of the night for months, ever since I took him away from his delightful friends, in his happy school, where he had merrily trotted in every day, lunchbox a-swinging. He was now suddenly going to be abandoned in an enormous institution, with five times the number of pupils, all speaking a language that resembled English, but had weird undertones and different phrases. How on earth was my shy, timid little lad going to cope?

Of course my fears where totally irrational and this had only been brought on because at the age of 13, I had moved with my parents, leaving my two older sisters behind in Merseyside, and relocated to Essex where my father had been given a promotion. At the age of 13, you are not rational. You are not compassionate. You are not at all reasonable, and the last thing on earth you want to do is leave your friends. To say I took it badly was an understatement. I was filled with rage. I couldn't bear the Essex accent, and I purposely spoke in an extremely strong Scouse accent which nobody understood (probably not even Scousers, as I actually couldn't do it very well).

I hated school and only went to registration so I could convert former model students to bunk off with me behind garages and smoke cigarettes, which I hated doing too.

I was in a terrible way.

The only way I could think of to make my parents realise how much I wanted to go back was to run away.

So one Sunday evening, as the top 40 counted down on Radio One, I slipped into my mother's handbag and stole some cash, announced to them that I was going round to a friend's house, which, as I hadn't even shown an interest in making any friends, pleased them immensely, and I hiked off in the direction of the train station.

I hadn't actually thought this through very well, and after asking a lovely elderly couple the correct way to the station, I decided it would be a good idea to talk to as many people as possible in case I later became featured on Crimewatch.

I managed to get the right train and headed off to London but once I had arrived there I had a long wait for the next train to Liverpool. I had a rather uncomfortable encounter with a dirt-encrusted hunchback in Euston station, who tried to entice me back to his cave until my train arrived. Then after several more episodes with fellow homeless people who latched onto me like a cluster of zombies hoping to sap my remaining life force, I decided I would sit tight in the ladies' toilet until my train arrived.

I arrived in Liverpool at some unearthly hour and was taken pity on by some very friendly middle-aged man, who let me share his cab over to the Wirral. And when I arrived at my familiar territory, I was exhausted. Although dawn was just breaking, I found a comfortable cornfield and nestled down to rest with my head on my Somerfield bag containing two pairs of knickers and some hair gel.

An hour or two later, I headed over to the bus stop where I knew all my friends would be waiting to go to school. I remember how excited I felt at seeing them all again and thought they would be so proud of me to have made it up here on my own. My plan completely backfired. My friends were horrified to see me; they couldn't believe that I could have done something so stupid; they had all been grilled by the police to see if they knew where I was and if they were in on the act, and their parents were livid.

What's more, my dad was on his way up to get me and I had strict instructions to stay with my friend's parents until he arrived.

Boy, was I in trouble.

After a heartfelt hug from my dad and an apology to my friend's parents for their lack of sleep, we headed back down to Essex in silence. I had never felt so guilty; I was mortified to have put my parents through such an awful ordeal. The whole unnecessary episode really made me grow up, and only a few weeks after that, I made some wonderful friends in Essex who to this day, almost 20 years later, are still my very best friends.

It's only now as a parent myself that I realise the horror of what I put my dear parents through, and so you can see why I had such a hang-up about moving my son from his former school.

As it happened, he fitted in perfectly.

Being only nine years old, he hadn't got to the stage where he was hanging out with friends after school in England. He quickly made hoards of new friends, most of them hailing from other countries themselves. Most people who live on the Sunshine Coast descend from other states or countries (for instance, the UK and New

Zealand and even South Africa) to take up residence here.

My relief was unbounded and it felt like a suitcase of bricks had been removed from my shoulders.

Where to Start?

My first impression at my son's school was how confident even the young children seemed to be. I know many of the children in his previous school in England would be quite shy if an adult were to approach them and ask directions, for instance. But I found almost all the children to be very forward, even to the point of being cheeky. So, a little concerned about this, I decided it would be a good idea, once my son had started at the school to help in the classroom and check out how they behaved during lessons. This put my mind at rest: although the kids could be a little on the cheeky side, they were also very polite, extremely helpful and exuded confidence beyond their years.

When you are searching for a good school to send your children to, you may be shocked to find that there is no OFSTED results table, and as we have always thought that the best way to judge a school, we found it more difficult to do so here.

NAPLAN

Australia has a different system to assess results, known as NAPLAN (National Assessment Programme for Literacy and Numeracy).

The students are tested in the following areas:

Literacy: reading and viewing, writing and spelling.

Numeracy: measurement and data, number and space.

The NAPLAN tests are for students in years 3, 5, 7 and 9, and they are taken nationally at the same time and on the same day, during the month of May.

The results of the test will be on your child's school report which you will receive in September. You can also find out the overall results for the school by logging onto their website.

Checking out a school on the web is good for information like that and it does offer a glimpse of the school curriculum and outline the running of the school. But remember they are only likely to advertise their best aspects and any underlying crime scenes wouldn't be mentioned. So it really is a case of checking schools out in person.

Day-Care Centres

Before the prep years, there are various Nursery schools, more commonly known as day-care centres or kindergartens, which are available for certified and accredited childcare. Children can start as early as six weeks in some centres and many offer after-school care for your older children too. But as in the UK, these centres vary dramatically, so taking the time to choose carefully is highly recommended.

Speaking from experience, my three-year-old daughter had been attending a nursery school in England since she was three months old, so I knew that although the change of surroundings may be a little hard at first, her social ability would help her find it a wonderful experience where she could interact with other children and generally enjoy playing and exploring. So I chose a day-care centre that was walking distance to our house. It looked clean enough and the staff seemed friendly, but to my astonishment, after the first couple of months my daughter actually became more timid. Although I had talked to the staff about my concerns, she still was not enjoying her time at the centre and had started to become very upset when I left her there, which was not in her character at all.

So one day, after I had left her clinging with a tear-soaked face to one of the teachers in her room, I crept along the outside fence and searched for a sizable hole in one of the panels where I could observe the children playing in the garden and still be hidden from sight. I was horrified to see that once I had left the building, my daughter, bottom lip still trembling and quite obviously not recovered from the separation from mum, was carelessly placed into the middle of the grass while the teacher walked off and took a call on her mobile phone.

I waited for a few moments to see if she would return to her and continue to console her, but instead she wondered off to talk to another staff member. My daughter looked truly distraught as the other children knocked into her as they played in groups around her, and although I knew no harm would come to her, I realised that this wasn't the sort of care I wanted for her.

Needless to say, she never returned to that centre. And I spent several weeks visiting other centres in search of one that offered more of a caring environment. Eventually I found an Early Learning Centre, which had a more structured routine. Since she started there, she has not had one morning of separation tears or uncharacteristic outbursts at home. She has become, once again, a confident happy little girl, which proves to me that not all day-care centres are alike.

One unusual point I should make, is that most of the centres charge for the full day, not by the hour or by the half day. If you receive government help with the fees (from Centrelink – covered in Chapter Nine) be aware that you have to keep your child's immunisation record up-to-date, otherwise your payments will cease. You will get a letter from Centrelink if your child is overdue for an immunisation, and you will have 21 days to have it done before the payments stop.

TOP TIP

Although you may feel like you are being pressured into having your child immunised and would rather not have it done or just postpone it, you can always make an appointment with your GP and express your concerns. Explain your reasons or your religious beliefs against certain immunisations, and they may be able to give you a conscientious objection form.

Day-care centres have flexibility in regards to drop off and pick up, but in my daughter's new centre, she must be there by nine o'clock as they like to have the children ready for lessons: creating fruit or animals with Play-Doh; painting the pathways with coloured water and cooking biscuits with teacher.

State Schools and Private Schools

Schools in Australia fall into two main categories:

1. Public (also known as government or state schools)

2. Independent (also known as private) and Catholic schools.

The private school fees vary, depending on which area you live in, but generally they are much lower than the private school fees in the UK, and many parents choose this option when they decide to emigrate, as they see this avenue as the ultimate in education. There are still other costs to consider, for instance expensive uniforms, games kit and equipment, plus school excursions to more exotic destinations than that of state schools.

When your child first attends a state school, it may come as a shock to you when you first receive your book list form. As with British schools, you are required to buy your children's school uniform, but at the moment you are also responsible for textbooks, exercise books, dictionaries and all school stationery. The cost for this is approximately $130 for the year.

They do make it easy and supply you with a list at the beginning of term four, so all you have to do is fill in what you need and pay up at the office. The costs for school excursions and some sporting activities will also need to be covered.

There is also a *voluntary contribution* to pay; this can vary from school to school, from under $100 to over 300 dollars, depending on where you live. These contributions are for the year ahead and go towards a range of school resources like data projectors for each classroom, interactive whiteboards and coffee and bickies for the teachers' morning tea. I jest, of course.

The Victorian Government introduced the *School Start Bonus* in 2006, available to eligible families who have a student entering into prep or making the transition to Year 7. The bonus is given in the form of a payment voucher which you can take to the post office – along with ID – and redeem for cash. This will help pay for the start-up costs of primary and secondary school, like school and sporting uniforms, school bags and other items.

School Holidays

The biggest difference is that the main six-week summer holidays are in December and the new school year starts at the end of January, which takes a little getting used to, but actually works fantastically well because the children have loads of time to play with their Christmas toys and also spend most of their time messing about in the swimming pool or on the beach.

There are four school terms a year (Tasmania is an exception, with only have three terms) divided into two semesters and they are *generally* around the following dates, although each state can differ by a couple of days:

1. Summer term	23 January – 7 April
2. Autumn term	19 April – 23 June
3. Winter term	11 July – 22 September
4. Spring term	9 October – 15 December

There are normally about five 'student-free' days too, mainly on the first day of term.

Private schools have longer holiday periods, but these are still taken around the same time.

Public Holidays

The first six months of the year seems to have a public holiday every other week, so a great tip if you are considering using a childcare centre, is to try to avoid having Mondays as one of your child's days. They always close on public holidays but you will still get billed for it, plus you will have to find other arrangements for your little one if you still have to work. Here's a list of public holidays:

- Australia Day – January 26 (and if it falls on a weekend, you get the Monday as a holiday)
- Good Friday and Easter Monday
- ANZAC Day – April 25
- Labour Day – (differs in each state)
- Queen's Birthday – June 12

If you accidentally call a public holiday a bank holiday (which does not exist in Australia), most Australians know what you mean.

TOP TIP

Different states have their own public holiday dates and schools often close for other unusual days too, like show days. This is where a local town may have a mini festival in a large field or sports centre – don't get too enthused, they can be full of toothless oddballs. The good thing is, you can take the opportunity to take the kids to out-of-town attractions – like one of the many "Worlds" (Seaworld, Dreamworld, Movieworld etc) on the Gold Coast... and you will almost have the whole place to yourself!

School Admission Ages for Each State

It is compulsory for children to start Year 1 in their sixth year, but before that, each state has a different system for the early years. They are all full-time and mainly play-based, but not compulsory.

Queensland

Queensland schools have introduced a *'prep'* (preparatory) year for five year olds; before 2007 it was referred to as *preschool*. The children start their first year in prep, in the January of the year of their fifth birthday, if it falls before June 30.

Then they go into Year 1 and stay in the same school until the end of Year 7, and go to high school in Year 8.

South Australia

In South Australian schools, the first year of schooling is called *reception*.

The child can start reception class in the new term following their fifth birthday.

High school is started in Year 8.

Western Australia

Western Australia refer to the first year as *pre-primary*. Children start this at the beginning of the year, if they turn five before June 30.

They start high school in Year 8.

Victoria

Victorian Schools also have *prep*. The child will start in the year of their fifth birthday if it falls before April 30. They stay in primary school until the end of Year 6, and go to high school in Year 7.

New South Wales

New South Wales Schools have *kindergarten*, which they can start at the beginning of the school year if they are aged five on or before July 31.

They start high school in Year 7.

Tasmania

Tasmania also has *prep* and the children start when their fifth birthday falls before January 1.

Their high school starts in Year 7.

Australian Capital Territory

ACT refers to it as *kindergarten*. Children needed to have turned five by April 30 to join the year.

Their high school starts in Year 7.

Northern Territory

In the Northern Territory it is known as *transition*.

The children should be five by June 30, and then there is a continuous intake for children after their fifth birthday.

They start middle school in Year 7 and high school in Year 10.

Seriously Strange School Stuff

A strange term I came across when my son first started his school was when the teacher told me to make sure I had enough 'contact' for all of his books. I don't know about you, but I had never heard of this. It turns out Contact is a brand name for what we would cover our kids' books in, a bit like when we used to use old wallpaper or sometimes comic book pages to decorate the front and back cover. I, of course, looked dull-witted at the teacher until she explained it to me. How many more times must I look so gormless?

Be aware when buying school shoes that most of the Aussie kids wear black (or white) trainers (known as joggers here) as opposed to the smart Velcro/tie-up type shoes in England. This is because in some schools the children don't change into a conventional PE kit, but for unknown reasons, they have their sweaty PE lessons in their uniforms and therefore won't be changing shoes to go on a 200 metre sprint.

My son, whom I cursed with a hereditary tortoise gene, wasn't best pleased with me when he consistently dragged his clubbed feet into a last place defeat in every race due, partially, to his cumbersome shoes. Consequently I was forced to buy him a new pair of joggers after only a few weeks. Unfortunately, it made no difference and he still continually stumbles in last.

Once, when I was waiting outside the school classroom to pick up my son at the end of the day, I remarked to a fellow mum on how neat the teacher's handwriting was.

"Arrr yeah, they're good at that Queensland cursive stuff in this school!" came the reply.

I don't know about you, but when you are constantly bombarded with odd phrases, strange expressions and unexpected answers, I had had just about enough of feeling like the new girl.

So I replied in a hopeful, "Yeah, err that's got to be good hasn't it?" then raced home and Googled the phrase 'Queensland Cursive', praying I hadn't sounded like a complete fool.

Here is what I found out: each state has a different handwriting style (I know, don't laugh). If your child has not yet started school, you can contact the office to see which style is being taught in the school to give them a head start in their writing style.

- In **Victoria**, they teach the Victorian Modern Cursive Script
- In **South Australia** they teach South Australian Cursive
- The **Northern Territory** teaches Victorian Cursive Script
- **ACT** teaches ACT Cursive Script
- **Tasmania** teaches Tasmanian Cursive Script

- **Queensland** teaches Queensland Cursive Script
- **Western Australia** teaches Modern Cursive Script
- **New South Wales** teaches New South Wales Foundation Style

I have included websites for all the state education departments in the resources page, so you can check out any other odd anomalies before you arrive.

Although they have bountiful tuck-shops, most state schools do not have a canteen and therefore no school dinners. So you will be met with blank looks when you screw up your face and reminisce of lumpy school semolina. The hanging flesh from your upper arms can no longer be referred to as 'dinner lady arms' – but can be replaced with 'tuck-shop lady arms'.

TOP TIP

The tuck shop comes in handy when you have had just about enough of preparing packed lunches every day. Just remember to pack an ice-pack in the lunch box, as they stay in the kids' bags all morning, not in a fridge.

I recall putting my son's shoes through the washing machine one Friday after school, as there was a terrible smell wafting around them. Only to uncover a half opened yoghurt at the bottom of his school bag under dog-eared newsletters. Clearly it had been there for several days. As I ventured nearer, the stench was eye-watering and I can only describe it as though someone with a ghastly stomach ache had been sick into a tramp's sock.

Resources

School Jargon Translations

Australian	English
Day care	Nursery *
Contact	Sticky-back book covering
Bubbler	Drinking fountain
Popper	Small carton of juice
White Out	Tippex
Textas	Felt-tip pens
Reader	Reading book

* 'Nursery' in Australia means garden centre

Schools Information

www.naplan.edu.au
(info on the national schools NAPLAN tests)

www.privateschoolsdirectory.com.au
(find private schools in your area)

www.australianschoolsdirectory.com.au
(find state schools in your area)

State-Specific School Information

www.det.act.gov.au (Australian Capital Territory)
www.det.nsw.edu.au (New South Wales)
www.schools.nt.edu.au (Northern Territory)
www.education.qld.gov.au (Queensland)
www.decs.sa.gov.au (South Australia)
www.education.tas.gov.au (Tasmania)
www.det.wa.edu.au/education (Western Australia)

9: Work Farce

Now the next thing, I suppose, is the reality of work – to pay for your new lifestyle. When we had visited our new friends from the guest book, they had given us so much information that we weren't aware of. For instance, it turns out that if you hold a residency visa, although you can't claim unemployment benefit for two years, you can claim other benefits, like childcare benefit and help with your rent, if you are on a low income.

The first step was to apply for a tax file number, easily done online, and then we were to visit our local Centrelink to apply for whatever else we were entitled to.

The very helpful chap in the office asked us to fill out various forms as he took photocopies of our passports, and as we had been entitled to benefits since the day we landed in Australia, we were presented a week or so later, with a cheque for over a thousand dollars.

Now, although Max had been working as a barber, and had his own shop for over 12 years, he was somewhat hesitant to carry on with this job any longer. He felt that now was the perfect time to embark on a new career, but as he also felt he had been off work long enough, and as he got three job offers in as many days, he decided for the time being to take a job working in a barber's shop in a local shopping mall, only a five-minute drive from our house, and only four days a week. This gave him time to look round for something more permanent – and preferably not cutting hair.

That just left me. As I mentioned before, I was aware that I couldn't carry on my chiropody in Australia, not only because my qualification wasn't recognised, but the actual title 'chiropodist' wasn't even heard of. Imagine my disbelief when thumbing through the Yellow Pages I found no mention of my profession. Instead, after chimney sweeps it went straight to chiropractors. Incidentally, there were only four chimney sweeps – so don't try and base your visa application on that. I had had a good standing in the community in England and was often approached to sign applications for passports as a professional person. To suddenly be downgraded to having no qualifications, with no chance of doing my job again unless I was willing to study for several years at university, was not encouraging.

But, it didn't deter me. I decided I would go forth and check out another form of earning money: the change would do me good, and I'm always ready to embark on something new.

I decided to apply for a telemarketing job, selling holidays on the coast. The hours were great (school-run friendly), it was only a five-minute drive from home, the money wasn't bad, and there was lots of potential to make extra cash bonuses too. After a rather casual interview, where the supervisor and her staff were all wearing pyjamas – I was presuming for charity, I was offered a position.

I remember feeling extremely nervous as I entered the office for the first time. For a start, I didn't know what everyone was going to be wearing: were pyjamas an everyday occurrence in this office? So I opted for a casual/smart look, and took an amusing hat in my bag, in case being stupid was a necessity.

I got there at the appointed time, and found the other staff members really helpful. First I had a couple of forms to fill in, and then 'Billy' gave me the low down on how to deal with difficult customers.

I was then temporarily placed next to a couple of old hands, who looked like they had come straight off the set of a Two Ronnies sketch. They could easily have passed for men in heavily applied red lipstick, and obscurely patterned nylon-cum-polyester dresses, but I was shocked and amazed at how naturally gifted they were, as on call after call they enticed unsuspecting customers into securing an 'unmissable holiday deal'. I watched them in awe, imagining that this could really be fun.

About an hour after that, Billy decided it was my turn to have a go… and that is when the job turned from a fun-loving place to work to the heinous pit of hell.

I had never imagined how uncomfortable and cringe-making it is to phone random people from who-knows-where and try and sell them a holiday they quite obviously do not want. I carried on pursuing person after person, using the daily script Billy had presented me and getting absolutely nowhere.

Yet, of course, it is in a highly motivated environment, so you are obliged to sit there with a permanent cheesy grin on your face even though your cheek bones are starting to twitch with pain, giving high fives to other team members who randomly pass your desk.

At last, lunch time arrived, and not a second too early. I flew outside to get some fresh air, and massage my cramped cheeks as I had been wearing an expression not unlike that of The Joker from Batman. Many more of my new work colleagues had begun to join me and most of them were there for more of a cigarette break (or 'smoko' as it's joyously known) than lunch. I watched them appear one by one: a sour-looking middle aged woman with a purple nose, a couple of extremely obese women wearing flamboyant tracksuit bottoms and a chap in his late thirties, who from the side looked quite normal, but when confronted face on, appeared to have one eye the size of a peanut and one the size of a kitchen clock.

My next thought was that maybe I should just make a bolt for it. I could see my car beckoning me in the distance, but everyone had already stubbed out their nicotine-induced lunch and had started to make their way back to the office. While I hesitated, a friendly girl in a wheelchair had ridden up to me and seemed keen to accompany me back to our desks. I glanced back over to my car and the last escape to freedom, but decided I couldn't deny this girl conversation and, after a hopelessly embarrassing moment in which I got in one of those open-plan lift affairs with her to climb two steps – reluctantly went back for the second half of my awful day.

Twenty useless phone calls later, I glanced at my watch. Only a horrifying 15 minutes had passed, which meant I still had 1 hour 45 minutes to go... this was not good.

I concocted a plan that I would go to the bathroom at half hourly intervals, with the hope that I could lose at least 15 minutes that way. This worked. It gave me something to aim for, in the same way a twitching alcoholic has to take his recovery one day at a time.

When half past two finally arrived, Billy beavered over to say I had done superbly well and that he hadn't expected me to make any sales on the first day. He also informed me that all the fun would start tomorrow, when I would make sales. I smiled as much as I could without looking like a dead horse... while in my mind I was repeating his words:

"Fun? Fun?"

I bade everyone farewell with my last trickle of enthusiasm, (some of them were doing overtime, would you believe?) and with the usual jolly high five scenario, shouted,

"See you tomorrow..."

"Like hell," I muttered under my breath, as I vanished out of the door and raced to the car park.

Needless to say, I never returned. I did have one more stomach churning phone call to make the next morning though, to Billy, to tell him of my rather sudden departure. Luckily, he was unavailable so I was able to pass the message on and didn't have to use my elaborate excuse that I had been working on throughout the night.

I don't regret my six-hour career as a telemarketing girl, but I do take an extra minute to be a little more compassionate to the folks who do that job now.

First Things First

Most people immigrating to Australia have a vague idea of the type of work they are going to do. Some people have jobs lined up before they get here. Good for them – that way their employer can fill them in on how to go about starting off.

But for others, us included, there are some basic steps that need to be followed and *in the right order*.

Before you head off down to the job agency or start frantically circling ads in the newspaper, get yourself a Tax File Number (TFN).

Tax File Number

This nine-digit number is really important, because without it you will be paying the maximum tax on your wages, which at the moment is 46.5%... gulp.

To get a TFN, you need to complete an application or enquiry for individuals – a NAT 1432 form – which you can get from your local tax office, some newsagents or the Tax Office website (the address is in the resources page).

You have to physically take it into the office when you have completed the form, as they require *original* documents to prove your identity.

TOP TIP
It is essential that you make getting a Tax File Number one of the first jobs you do when you land in Oz, as you must allow 28 days from the date of application to receiving it.

The next step is to get yourself registered with *Centrelink*, especially if you are arriving with a family.

Centrelink Stuff

Centrelink is a service run by the government and provides information on social security; employment; education; training and health and family matters along with many other things.

As long as you hold a permanent residency visa, you will be entitled to make a claim for childcare benefit, which is similar to the family allowance in the UK.

If you are looking into childcare facilities – as long as you intend to work and are actively looking for work, or study – they may be able to help with a percentage of the childcare fees.

They will also advise you on any other entitlements that you could claim, for instance, help with rental payments.

Please note, though, that you will not be entitled to employment benefit for the first two years in Australia.

TOP TIP

If your combined income is below $40,000 per annum (that's $39,999) you will automatically be entitled to a concession or Health Care Card.

Health Care Card

A Health Care Card may appear to be a little flimsy cardboard slip but it is actually extremely helpful. It entitles you to:

- Commonwealth health concessions
- Concessions offered by private companies
- Reduced cost medicines under the Pharmaceutical Benefits Scheme (PBS)
- State and local government concessions such as:
  - Health-care costs including ambulance, dental and eye care
  - public transport costs
  - water rates
  - energy and electricity bills

So it really is worth taking a trip down to your local Centrelink.

Super

Superannuation (or just 'super' as its known) is a way of saving money while you are working to help fund your retirement. Basically, it is the Aussie pension scheme.

TOP TIP

Australia's financial year runs from July 1 – June 30. So the end of June is a great time to grab some fantastic bargains at the shopping centres at the 'end of financial year' sales!

Rather than rely on social security, the government is aiming to steer most Australians towards being able to self-fund their retirement, although the state pension will still be available for those who need it.

Super can get extremely complex, and there have been many books written solely on the subject, so for me to try and explain it in one part of a chapter is inconceivable. So, as this book is meant to be a light-hearted approach to immigrating, I won't bog you down with tons of weighty information. Here is a taster.

Most employers are required to contribute super on behalf of their employees. This is called employer-funded super. It is under the Superannuation Guarantee (SG) Act which, since July 1 2002, has been set at 9%. These contributions are known as employer-funded contributions. Conditions apply so check your eligibility with your employer.

Relying on your employer's contribution may not enable you to live the lifestyle you require once you hit retirement age, so an option is to start paying employee-funded contributions: additional amounts into your Super fund to help provide a higher income when you are retired.

If you are self-employed, you can make your own contributions and they can also be tax-deductible up to certain limits.

By making spouse contributions the working spouse can contribute a certain amount into the non-working or low-earning spouse's super fund and be entitled to a tax rebate.

TOP TIP

There are dozens of companies specialising in super. Many of them also specialise in certain professions, so it's best to look into it when you gain employment.

Many Australians have a financial adviser, an expert in superannuation planning, as it is becoming increasingly complicated. So as a commercial on TV at the moment phrases it: "You look after your life, we'll look after your super!" What a great idea.

Resources

Tax File Number

www.ato.gov.au (click 'individual' and follow the links to apply for a Tax File Number)

The number to call to order a tax file number application form over the phone (in Australia) is: 1300 720 092

Essential Links

www.centrelink.gov.au
www.ato.gov.au/super

Employment Agencies

www.careerone.com.au
www.mycareer.com.au
www.linkme.com.au
www.seek.com.au

10: In Need of Medical Attention

Perhaps it was the stress of the move, the excitement of our new life or just that I was becoming idle with no job to go to but I was beginning to feel quite fatigued, sometimes nodding off like a frail old granny in the afternoon before picking up the children. It wasn't until I felt the first waves of nausea one morning that I realised there was a possibility I could be pregnant.

The test proved positive and I was thrown onto an emotional rollercoaster. We hadn't totally ruled out another baby, but having lived only six weeks in a new country, I had so many concerns I just didn't know where to begin. Where was the nearest hospital? Or even the nearest doctor (I still hadn't registered with one). Would I have to pay medical expenses? How were we going to pay for the little blighter? Max was only working part-time and I was absolutely no use as I was a pale jade colour, retching down the loo most of the time. And, more importantly, what was my mum going to say?

I know now that it was just my hormones, but I have never felt more lonely and homesick. I longed for my friends to talk to and all the baby shops I was so used to: Mothercare World, Boots and the little baby shop in Rayleigh where I used to buy all my daughter's beautiful dresses. I felt like I knew nobody and had no support network around me. Don't get me wrong, my husband is completely at home with most 'women's things', but sometimes you just need a girlfriend to talk these things over with.

So when my son announced that he had a new boy arrive in his class from Wales, I raced down to the school gates. She didn't know it yet, but this boy's mother was going to be my new best friend.

Nicola turned out to be an absolute treasure. She had a fantastic sense of humour and we immediately gelled. We spent hours talking, in a way only women can do, and I felt intensely happy to have found a friend. She and her husband had three boys, and we all spent many long afternoons at our house, enjoying our huge pool as the time went on and summer made its presence felt. My morning sickness had started to lessen, and everything was starting to look much rosier.

Until the fateful fortnight of late August, early September.

My two cats had been blissfully enjoying the winter sun, and they had become quite accustomed to the mystifying squawks of unusual birds and wildlife. I had constructed a couple of comfy beds for them to sleep in, which Aubrey loved, but Fluffer, after close inspection and many long sniffs, had no intention of nesting in. And so she found herself a little alcove in the sun covered by some wistful ferns.

One day, after calling her for breakfast, she didn't come in. This wasn't really unusual; sometimes she'd wait until Aubrey had eaten, then she would dine alone. I always thought of it as some sort of hierarchy, as Aubrey was the dominant male.

So it wasn't until she still hadn't been back for lunch that I started my search for her. I discovered her poor matted body, barely breathing, under a palm tree leaf. She had obviously crawled under it with her dwindling energy to get out of the scorching sun. After I'd placed her frail body into her cat basket, leaning away from her feeble attempts to spit and hiss at me as if I were deliberately trying to murder her, I drove her to the nearest vet.

By the state of her, she looked as though she'd been attacked by something fairly large, aggressive and froth-mouthed, but following an inspection by the vet, he told me that he had uncovered a tick.

"Oh, blimey, is that all?" I said with a sigh of relief, but unfortunately as the vet informed me, making her better wasn't just a simple case of removing the tick.

Oh no, the ticks in Queensland are notoriously deadly. The one she was carrying was known as a paralysis tick: among the most dangerous parasites that can affect your pet. The horrid little terror sucks blood from the host animal and in so doing secretes saliva full of toxins, which are absorbed, causing paralysis and poisoning. How very pleasant. The vet administered an anti-toxin and kept her there for the rest of the day under observation, but Fluffer didn't recover and was put to sleep later that evening.

The next few days were inevitably sad, not just at the loss of our beloved cat, but also at the thought of how much we'd spent on bringing her over. Still, I had learned a valuable lesson which I want to share with you: that you should always keep your animals protected with some type of tick and flea treatment and check them regularly for those perilously evil little blighters.

Unfortunately, the week continued with more unpleasant events. I woke early on Saturday morning and found myself in the process of losing the baby.

I won't go into graphic detail, but I was just over 12 weeks pregnant, so it was not like having a normal monthly distribution.

My husband drove me down to the doctor's surgery and after a big hug with a lovely nurse, and some paracetamol, I was allowed home. Luckily, when I went for an investigative scan a few days later, I found I didn't need to have a curate. I wasn't entirely sure what this entailed exactly, but I was immensely glad it didn't apply to me.

Back at the school gates on Monday morning, I had the uncomfortable job of untelling everyone that I'd told I was pregnant, which came as a huge sadness to my dear friend Nicola, who was about to announce the news that she had just found out, on Saturday morning, that she too was expecting.

I don't know who I felt worse for, her or me. I was as happy for her as possible, and we went out together for a nice cup of tea, which of course, is the obvious thing for anyone from Britain to do in that situation.

Over our cuppa, and incidentally a sumptuously pleasant scone, Nicola was telling me how she felt very unsettled and extremely homesick. I explained to her that I knew exactly how dire she felt, as I had the same emotions when I first found out that I was pregnant, and all I wanted to do was run home in a panicky terror. I mentioned that I couldn't appreciate our beautiful new surroundings, as even the views from our backyard made me feel like regurgitating copious amounts of stomach bile.

I also told her that she would soon feel better, and to just let this time tick on a bit. While we were having this heart to heart, I was positioned facing a bus stop and on the back of a stationary but vibrating bus was an enormous picture of Steve Irwin with conquering arms and an over-enthusiastic grin, advertising his infamous zoo. For some reason, I found myself strangely absorbed by it, but as the bus trundled off to its next destination, I thought nothing of it.

When my husband arrived back from work later that evening, I was eager to tell him about Nicola and her pregnancy and her homesickness, when he stopped me abruptly and gave me the news that Steve Irwin had been killed in North Queensland, while filming a documentary for his daughter.

I was distraught. I don't know whether it was because we were living only a stone's throw from the zoo, or whether it was because we had children the same age and therefore could relate to how his wife would be feeling, or the fact that I'd tried to be so strong with all the other sad little episodes of late, but I just broke down and cried.

Once again, that overwhelming urge to pack up and go home hit me; everything seemed to be going wrong. I am always an optimist, but I just couldn't seem to muster any enthusiasm.

A week later, after sobbing uncontrollably through the Steve Irwin memorial, Nicola announced she was leaving to go back to Wales.

This was a huge turning point for me; I could either lie down and become more depressed by the minute, or get out there and show Australia what I had to offer.

I chose the latter, and with my new-found enthusiasm... I went to help at the school fête.

Medicare

After this little episode and many visits to the doctor, I learnt a lot about how the Medicare system works and as it is very different to the NHS, I thought it would definitely be worth dedicating a chapter to it.

Medicare, originally called Medibank, was introduced by the Whitlam Labour Government in July 1975. It had a rather hostile reception and over the years considerable changes have been made, but in 1984, the Hawke government changed its title to Medicare and along with that came the introduction of what can be considered the current Medicare system.

Medicare is intended to provide affordable treatment by doctors and in public hospitals for all citizens and permanent residents.

Residents with a Medicare card can receive subsidised treatment from medical practitioners and public hospital treatment and accommodation is free of charge. This is funded through the Commonwealth-State Health Care Agreements.

So basically, as soon as you get here with your permanent residency visa embedded in your passport, get yourself down to your local Medicare office and get registered. Too easy.

Here is a list that Medicare provides benefits for:

Out-of-Hospital Services

- Consultation fees for doctors, including specialists
- Tests and examinations by doctors needed to treat illnesses, including x-rays and pathology tests
- Eye tests performed by optometrists

- Most surgical and other therapeutic procedures performed by doctors
- Some surgical procedures performed by approved dentists
- Specified items under the Cleft Lip and Cleft Palate Scheme
- All associated treatment costs when you are treated as a public patient (registered with Medicare) in a public hospital.

You can choose the doctor you want for out-of-hospital services.

In-Hospital Services

Public patient: If you are admitted to a public hospital as a public (Medicare) patient, the treatment you receive by the doctors and specialists will be nominated by the hospital. You will not be charged for the treatment or the aftercare by the treating doctor.

Private patient: If you are a private patient in a public or private hospital, you can choose which doctor you would like to treat you. Medicare will pay 75% of the fee for services and procedures provided by the doctor treating you. If you have private health insurance some or all of the balance can be recovered.

You will be charged for hospital accommodation and other things such as theatre fees and medicines. These costs can also be covered by private health insurance.

What Medicare Doesn't Cover

- Ambulance services
- Glasses and contact lenses
- Dental examinations and treatment (but some essential dental surgery *is* covered)
- Hearing aids, prostheses and other appliances

- Physiotherapy, occupational therapy, speech and eye therapy, chiropody (because it's not even recognised here – not that I'm bitter), podiatry, chiropractic services and psychology
- Medicines
- Home nursing
- Acupuncture (unless part of a doctor's consultation)
- Medical and hospital costs incurred overseas
- Medical services which are not clinically necessary
- Surgery for cosmetic reasons only
- Funeral costs or medical repatriation
- Accommodation and medical treatment in a private hospital
- Accommodation and medical treatment as a private patient in a public hospital
- Examinations for life insurance, superannuation or membership of a friendly society

But you can arrange private health insurance to cover many of these services and I have listed a number of websites for you to check out on the resources page.

The best thing to do, when looking for a GP in your new designated area is to find one that has the '100% bulk billed' sign, as this would be a real bonus.

TOP TIP

If you have an up-to-date prescription, you can also order your contact lenses online at
www.eyecontacts.com.au
This is quite an economical way of doing it, but some restrictions apply. For example, if you are cursed with astigmatism, as I am, then your lenses won't be available and you will have to go down the optometrist route. Luckily, since I have been living here, good old Specsavers has arrived, so you can just carry on from where you left off!

Bulk Billing

This is a payment option under the Medicare system, where the health service provider is paid 85% of the scheduled fee directly by the government by billing the patient via their Medicare card. Which means when you've finished your appointment, just visit the reception desk and sign a form and you won't have to part with any cash.

The service provider only receives 85% of the fee, but avoids the costs and risks of billing and debt collection. However, many of the surgeries, like mine for instance, have stopped offering this service now.

The alternative is for the service provider to collect the fee directly from the patient, after the appointment. Then what you do is to pop along to your Medicare office, of which there are many, and fill out a claim form which enables you to claim back 85% of the scheduled fee, or 100% in the case of GP services. A bit more of a palaver, but something you learn to live with.

Donating Blood

All of Australia's blood donors are voluntary and unpaid. Donors give blood because they want to do something very special for the community and they know they are helping their fellow Aussies in a practical way. Australia is also one of a handful of countries which is self-sufficient in blood supply; in other words, they give enough blood to meet the needs of the community. Another factor that contributes to Australia having one of the safest blood supply systems in the world are the regulations around which eligibility to give blood is determined. And this is what prompted me to write this paragraph.

You cannot donate blood if you:

- are under 16 (under 18 in Tasmania or the Northern Territory)
- are over 70
- have recently had a tattoo
- are pregnant
- gave birth recently
- have a serious heart condition
- are low in Iron

...and how about this one:

- lived in the UK for over six months between 1980 and 1996!

This final requirement is related to concerns about variant CJD or Mad Cow Disease.

How very strange. Does that mean that we are all constantly infecting each other with our mad blood in Britain?

More in-depth information on this subject can be found by manoeuvring around the website listed on the resources page.

Need an Ambulance? Call the Ambos!

Firstly, try and remember that it's no good calling 999 in Australia. All you'll get is a message to say you haven't dialled correctly. The number to call for the emergency services is triple zero (000) or 112 from a mobile phone.

Community Ambulance Cover (CAC) replaced the former Queensland Ambulance Subscription Scheme and ambulance transport charges on July 1 2003. Quite simply, CAC means that all Queensland residents are automatically covered for the cost of ambulance transportation anywhere, anytime across Australia.

CAC gives certainty of funding to the Queensland Ambulance Services by spreading the cost across the community.

A charge of 29.877 cents a day or $109.05 a year will apply to each electricity sale arrangement and it will appear on your electricity bill under 'other charges and credits' unless an exemption has been obtained.

As CAC only applies to people who have their principal place of residence in Queensland, the ambulance service recommends that interstate visitors should contact their own state or territory ambulance service, or their health fund, to enquire about options for coverage in Queensland. International visitors should arrange travel insurance.

If you are travelling interstate, you must be able to prove that you have your principal place of residence in Queensland, for instance your driver's license, so that you are covered. If you cease to be a Queensland resident, you will no longer be covered and as Queensland is the only state to have CAC, you will find using the ambulance service in any other state quite costly.

An example of this would be in South Australia, which operates a 'user-pays' system. This is where the fee for the ambulance is payable by the patient transported to or from a hospital, surgery or other place whether or not he or she consented to the provision of the service.

The cost of an emergency ambulance is around $600 depending on the priority at the time of dispatch.

In Victoria, they operate an ambulance membership and for an affordable fee, you are covered for all ambulance transport and ambulance treatment Australia-wide. It can cost you upwards of $5,000 for a trip in an ambulance, so it is well worth considering.

All the other states and territories (WA, TAS, NT, ACT and NSW) all charge for their ambulance services and there are not many exemptions to the fees. Some of the states have reciprocal agreements with each other (for instance ambulance membership) but they all suggest having cover from a health-care fund company of your choice. Most of the companies offer 'Ambulance Cover Only' options. I have listed all the ambulance websites for each state in the resources page.

Baby Capsules

Another service the ambos provide is what's known as baby capsule hire. A baby capsule is the first car seat a child has, up to about the age of six months (or nine kilograms). Hiring one can be very cost effective and they have fully trained staff available to fit it in your car, so that your baby is safe and comfortable. Even if you choose to buy your own, if you call them for an appointment they will ensure that it is fitted correctly too.

You can hire baby capsules from one week to six months, and they also cater for twins, triplets and (perish the thought) quads.

TOP TIP

If you were considering bringing a child's car seat over from the UK, note that it will not comply with Aussie standards. I brought two car seats over, both bought from Mothercare World, but I couldn't use them. Australian vehicles have a unique 'top tether strap anchorage system'– which only Australian standard approved child restraints are compatible with.

Here is an easy guide to select your child restraint, though be aware that this varies fractionally from state to state.

Type of restraint	Weight (approx)	Age (approx)
Infant capsule (rear-facing) or infant restraint	Less than 8kg	0–6 mnths
Rear- or forward-facing infant restraint	8–12kg	6 mnths–1 yr
Forward-facing child restraint with built-in harness	8–18kg	6 mnths–4 yrs
Booster seat with either H-harness or secured adult seatbelt	14–26kg	4–7 yrs
An H-harness can be used with or without a booster seat for a child up to 32kg		

Resources

General Information

www.donateblood.com.au
www.medicareaustralia.com.au

Ambulance Services by State

www.saambulance.com.au (South Australia)
www.ambulance.nsw.gov.au (New South Wales)
www.ambulance.qld.gov.au (Queensland)
www.ambulance.net.au (Western Australia)
www.ambulance.act.gov.au (Australian Capital Territory)
www.ambulance.vic.gov.au (Victoria)
www.stjohnnt.com.au (Northern Territory)
www.dhhs.tas.gov.au (Tasmania)

Private Health Insurance

www.ahm.com.au
www.mbf.com.au
www.medibank.com.au
www.nib.com.au
www.iselect.com.au (compares the health funds you select to save money)

11: That's Entertainment

It was all new to me, this helping at school malarkey, as I'd always been a working mum, so it came as a pleasant surprise to find hordes of other mums doing the same thing. It was only when I started chatting to them that I realised they were nearly all English! I wasn't going all out to find a load of new English friends, but during the weeks that followed, I found a couple of the most wonderful people I could ever have wished to meet.

Let me tell you, the Aussies know how to throw a school fête. Gone are the sedate days of the tombola, hook-a-duck, white elephant stalls, and the infamously rigged coconut shy.

Aussie school Fetes have huge action-packed rides with whizzing waltzers and thunderous roller coasters. We did have a little confusion with an elderly chap with beady eyes, wiry mutton chops and a great barrel chest, as he insisted he wanted to buy a ticket for the slippery dick. We were all set to call security, but it turns out that this is the name of the huge inflatable slide. Actually it's 'slippery dip', but he had a tongue like a cockatoo and numerous missing teeth.

We all decided, after bouts of raucous laughter, to make a date for a girls' night out. A week later we were all sitting in my backyard, under our tranquil Balinese cabana overlooking the luxurious swimming pool with its stylish underwater lights, the flawless moonlight dancing over the tall palms, sipping wine and swapping tales about our journeys over here. We all decided we were actually living the dream – it seemed like we were living a million dollar lifestyle, and yet I was still to secure myself a job.

As we were having such a great time, we should have stayed at our house but as we had all managed to rustle up babysitters, we decided to make the most of it and go out and have a dance. At first all went well; we caught the free courtesy bus to the Surf Club and we all danced and enjoyed the live band that was playing.

But as usual, I made the fatal mistake of underestimating how much wine I could drink and after dancing like a coma victim being poked with a cattle prod, I then spent the rest of the evening staring at the inside of a toilet as I heaved up most of my upper intestines.

Unfortunately that was not the end. After being found by two of my new friends, slumped, clammy and a pale green colour, they took me outside to get some fresh air, where I talked in tongues until they managed to get me back onto the courtesy bus and on our way home.

We were only about five minutes away from my house, so we thought we were home and dry, until another wave of nausea hit me. I heaved up another casket of chardonnay all over the steps of the bus. Needless to say, we were instantly shown off and left on the roadside, with me in the gutter.

At this point, I can only recite what my friends later told me, as I had now become an unconscious mass of arms and legs, a bit like someone who had sustained a sudden narcolepsy attack. Apparently we had a steady stream of concerned citizens who consisted of:

a) A handful of do-gooder passers-by with helpful hints on

hangovers

b) An off-duty paramedic who gave me a look of utter disgust

c) The orange-clad Street Angels, a voluntary organisation who keep drunks from vomiting on the streets – or something. They explained that I had better be moved quickly before the police arrived as they were giving out on-the-spot fines – all part of an anti-hooning campaign.

d) Some rather dubious looking characters in a 1970s Holden with intoxicating clouds of smoke bellowing out of the windows.

e) The police.

As one friend explained to the police that there was somebody on their way to pick us up and that a paramedic had helped me through the worst of my food poisoning, the other was holding me up as though I was a ventriloquist dummy. Then as they pulled away, she let go of me and I slumped face down into the earth.

The next morning I woke to find myself fully dressed, filthy and smelling of something poorly recycled. Max was off to work, but he had made it quite clear I was in trouble when he got home, and mentioned some reference to not being a teenager anymore. So I lay in bed, while the children watched DVD after DVD and slowly I recovered, attending regularly to the stream of phone calls from my new buddies that just wanted to poke fun at me in my fragile state.

So that was a good ice-breaker, and luckily, I now have some very good friends who I see regularly... although not for nights out, unless I am the designated driver.

The next few weeks went by quietly and with regular visits

from my mother-in-law, I slowly got myself into a happy little routine of life in another country. My children were a huge help, as I met more and more mums at swimming clubs and hockey training, and as they, too, all seemed to be from different states. It became apparent that not many people actually originated from the Sunshine Coast, which I found a great comfort as maybe I wasn't so alien after all.

After a further attempt at yet another one of my careers, which this time involved huge cartoon murals on children's walls – of which I did all of one (and for free) at my daughter's day-care centre – I discovered, this time with absolute joy that I was once again pregnant, and even the frightful morning sickness wasn't going to keep me from feeling rapturous.

Food, Glorious Food!

Aussie families love their barbeques. Many of the children's play parks have adjoining undercover barbeque huts, which are all free of charge. All you have to do is press a button and you immediately have hot cooking facilities. It is common to see many families spending a lazy Sunday parked under them while the children run and frisk about, playing cricket (which is why they are so damn good at the sport) climbing trees and generally larking about. Parents often have their children's birthday parties at these areas too. They decorate the huts with balloons and streamers and will cook up a sausage sizzle – a sausage wrapped in white bread and topped with either barbeque or tomato sauce... or both.

Fast Food Outlets

The main fast food outlets in Oz are all very similar to the UK. You can still have the same old KFC, McDonalds (Maccas) and Subway, but Burger King is now called Hungry Jack's and there aren't any Wimpy restaurants.

Noodle Box is a stir-fry noodle fast food chain, producing Asian and Eastern flavours, all made to order from the menu and served in a seemingly bottomless box for you to take away and enjoy. At present there are outlets located in Victoria, South Australia, Tasmania, Queensland and New South Wales.

Domino's Pizza is here, also *Pizza Hut*, but predominantly as a takeaway outlet. They seem to have a lot fewer dine-in restaurants than the UK where there is a *Pizza Hut* establishment in every shopping outlet and high street. There are nine in New South Wales, four in Victoria, four in Queensland and only one in South Australia. But never fear, there is an alternative... of sorts:

Sizzler seems to be the nearest thing to buffet-style casual dining restaurant there is in Australia. No bookings are needed and for a one-off price you can fill up on soups, salad, pasta, fresh fruit and desserts as many times as you are able to physically manage. If you prefer to have a meal cooked for you from the menu, they can do that as well. Kids under three eat free and older kids (up to 12) range from $4.95–$8.95, depending on their age. So it really is pretty good value.

Fasta Pasta has about 36 restaurants dotted around Queensland, Northern Territory, South Australia, Victoria and Western Australia. This is an Italian pasta restaurant, which serves a wide selection of delicious pasta at an affordable price. They use fresh farm eggs to make their pasta fresh – none of that dried stuff. We found we could get a pretty wholesome meal and the kids loved it too.

Restaurants are more or less the same as the UK. Your budget will dictate the quality, although if you have a passion for seafood, you're in for a real treat. I have never encountered prawns of such gigantic proportions, and they do not let you down on flavour.

BYO or *BYOB* (bring your own booze) restaurants are plentiful here. I know there are more and more of these sprouting up in the UK now but I first saw it here in Oz about 18 years ago. I thought then that it was a wonderful idea, making eating out a lot more affordable. Good old Aussies!

There are some down sides to eating in Oz though: on occasion, I would buy ready-meals in England – not those plasticy frozen ones, but Sainsbury's *Taste the Difference* or Tesco's *Finest* range. I shouldn't even mention *Marks & Spencer* as I'm actually dribbling at the thought and this is becoming torturous. Because, unfortunately, there doesn't seem to be a range of freshly cooked meals that you can simply heat up at home, and now I am forced to cook. Even Jamie Oliver would lose patience with me, as I lack any talent in the kitchen and my palate is about as finely honed as a garden gnome's.

Elevenses?

Terms I found to be frightfully English were 'morning tea' and 'afternoon tea'. Now we all know that a mid-morning cuppa is pretty much normal behaviour in England, but in Australia, it involves food more than a drink and it is actually a time of day.

You see workmen all dressed up in their huge sun-safe work gear, pausing at the most beautiful lookout points, eating their morning tea. At school, the children will actually stop everything and make time for their morning tea.

TOP TIP

If you ever get invited over by a friend for morning tea, never go empty handed; even if they are adamant you are not to bring anything. If, like me, you are incapable of baking anything even half fit for human consumption then you simply need to pop into Brumby's bakers and buy a couple of Danish pastries or Lamingtons (which have great appeal with senior citizens) unless you want to be scorned, or even worse, banished from morning tea invites forever.

The Tim-Tam Slammer

A packet of biscuits always goes down well, and if you really want to join in with the Aussies, you simply must experience a 'Tim-Tam Slammer'. Now the first time you are encouraged to join in with this tradition, you may find that your new-found friends fail to warn you of the catastrophic avalanche of melted chocolate which invariably can cascade over every item of clothing you have on. So there's your warning.

The idea of a 'Tim-Tam Slammer' is to use the Tim-Tam biscuit (this looks somewhat similar to the UK's Penguin biscuit) as a makeshift straw by biting off the two very ends of the biscuit and then sucking up your tea with it.

As soon as you feel the biscuit start to collapse in your fingers, you slam it into your mouth. For any chocolate lovers out there, and I'm guessing there are many, this is the single most delectable chocolate moment I have ever experienced and it is highly recommended.

Afternoon tea is usually around mid 'arvo', when the kids get in from school, although I am yet to be invited to one. Maybe it's because I baked something myself last

---

TOP TIP

Practise alone first! Tim-Tams are now available in the UK, but if you have difficulties finding them, practise with Penguin biscuits – and once you get the hang of it, you can impress people with your professionalism.

---

time I was invited to *morning* tea, and they are now either still recovering from the episode, or dead.

Health and Fitness

I once thought it would be a good idea to get up at the time when the cackling crows think you should be up, and unless you have blu-tac inserted into each ear it is very difficult to sleep through their resonating squawks.

So I dragged myself out of my comfy bed and squeezed my nether regions into a pair of Lycra shorts, which is a sight best not witnessed if you have any type of gastric reflux problems. I screwed my tangled mop of hair into a topknot, reached for my bottle-end glasses and headed out into dawn's morning light.

Of course what I didn't bargain on was that the streets swarmed with fit, sleek, triathlon style power walkers, all very bright and merry and happy to greet you on passing. But at that time in the morning, I not only try desperately to avoid any type of eye contact, conversations are definitely out.

So after only 15 minutes of painful hill walking, which made me drip from places I was unaware *could* perspire (am I alone with sweaty kneecaps?) I gave up on the whole fitness regime and jolly greetings, and headed back home for peace and quiet and a very long cold shower.

By lunchtime, I felt like I had been up for hours and I was ready for bed. I now know why so many Queenslanders go to bed so early, sometimes as early as 8.30pm.

So now I prefer to swim in my own pool at a more sensible time of 6.30am, with just the pretty lorikeets for company. And I go to bed at a normal *adult* hour, well after the children are all tucked up and snoring away.

Although there are many fitness centres and gyms around Australia, studies have shown that the country claims to have an obesity problem, with Australia coming in 21st on the world's fattest country chart, just ahead of the UK who is in the 28th slot, and well behind America, at 9th.[1] There still seem to be a lot of people getting out there and enjoying sport though.

It is not unusual for children to have two or three after-school sporting activities, but many adults join sports clubs too. Obviously the climate of Australia lends itself to making full use of the outdoor leisure activities, but many people I talk to try all types of new activities, maybe to burn off all those morning tea breaks!

So go on, get out there and try something new!

---

[1] Information sourced from forbes.com

Twisted TV

I hope no one comes over to Australia hoping for top quality TV!

The programmes themselves are definitely improving, but the number of commercial breaks on Channels Seven, Nine and Ten are monotonous to the point of insanity.

Not only are they shown every 10 minutes, they also have to be played immediately after the opening credits. Then, just to ensure the programme totally loses momentum they are played just before the last minute of an edge-of-your-seat cliffhanger.

It doesn't end there though; when programmes finish there is *no* commercial break. Instead, the next programme starts back to back with the last one. So the only time you do actually want one, so you can nip out and make a nice cuppa, they even manage to take that single luxury away.

Mercifully, the ABC (Australian Broadcasting Corporation) is owned and financed by the government, so it is a commercial-free zone. This also gives it a better quality of viewing and the programmes are not all imports from America. In fact they show an awful lot of British dramas and comedies, which can be very comforting. Thank you good old Beeb!

Some of the shows that are imported from overseas can suddenly just disappear or even completely change direction from the series you had been watching.

An example of this would be an American show called *Jericho* that we had been watching for about five weeks. We dutifully tuned in at the same time the following week, to find a completely different programme on – and no explanation. The programme was just axed and never spoken of again. And it really wasn't *that* bad.

Another time, during a season of *House*, we had been following the story every week and were quite *au fait* with the characters, when suddenly half the cast we had been watching disappeared and a whole new story line was introduced, from a series that had run previously. Still no explanation.

Luckily, over the past couple of years, a whole array of new digital channels have arrived. This has certainly improved TV viewing to some extent, if only because we have a wider variety of programmes. Of course if you're still not satisfied and want *more* channels, there is always the satellite route: *Foxtel* and *Austar*. After six months of *rugs-a-million* ads informing us that they have slashed rug prices *again*, you will gladly do anything to reclaim your sanity.

Although I sound anti-commercials, I have to say that a great many of them are highly amusing. Remember Chris Tarrant's TV show about bizarre worldwide commercials? Well, a great many came from Down Under.

Even in the car you are not safe. Imagine having the radio turned up high after singing along with *Bohemian Rhapsody*, when an advert comes on about erectile dysfunction, and how you can overcome it by using a nasal spray. Highly amusing – yet extremely uncomfortable when you have inquisitive kids in the car, or even worse, granny.

One other note is that there is no such thing as a TV licence, so you don't feel quite as duped when there is nothing worth watching.

Down on the Beach

Ok, so you've decided against watching the TV and instead chosen to embrace the Aussie way of life. On the beach.

You have probably heard about the phrase "Slip, Slop, Slap" (for those who haven't, it means *slip on a shirt, slop on the sunscreen and slap on a hat)* and this message is conveyed throughout Australia.

Kids at school will not be allowed to play out at lunchtime without a wide brimmed hat. They also have a saying "No hat, no play" – and they don't mince their words either.

Australia has the highest incidence of skin cancer in the world, so it really is important to listen to their message.

So once you are suitably factor-thirty-ed up and have hidden any other bare flesh from the UV rays, you are ready to hit the beach.

One of the most vital parts of enjoying the beach, especially if you are swimming, is to always stay on a lifeguard-patrolled beach. You will never have to go far to find one and they will always have an updated board with all the latest swimming conditions, water temperature, type of waves etc.

Beach Flags and Their Meanings

- **Half red/half yellow flag** – safe area to swim
- **Completely green flag** – good swimming conditions
- **Completely yellow flag** – unstable conditions
- **Completely red flag** – do not enter the water

Here is an easy way to memorise some safety rules: just remember the F-L-A-G-S.

- **Find** the **flags** and swim between them – the red and yellow flags mark the safest place to swim at the beach.

- **Look** at the safety signs: they help you identify potential dangers and daily conditions at the beach.
- **Ask** a surf lifesaver for advice – surf conditions can change quickly so talk to a surf lifesaver or lifeguard before entering the water.
- **Get** a friend to swim with you so you can look out for each other's safety and get help if needed. Children should always be supervised by an adult.
- **Stick** your hand up for help: if you get into trouble in the water, stay calm, raise your arm to signal for help. Float with a current or rip – don't try and swim against it.

And remember:

- Never swim on unpatrolled beaches.
- Never swim at night.
- Never swim under the influence of alcohol.
- Never run and dive into the water.
- Never swim directly after a meal.

Many of the surf clubs have excellent facilities and if you are interested in getting your kids into beach safety and surf lifesaving, then *Nippers* is the best place to do it. Every club around Australia offers a *Nippers* programme.

Nippers is open to children from the age of 5 through to 13. Not only is it a fun way for your child to enjoy the beach in a safe environment, it also offers children an educational pathway through the delivery of the SLSA Junior Development Program. This programme is designed to ensure children have fun at the beach while participating in lessons that will pave the way to them becoming a fully rounded participant in both lifesaving and sport.

RSL Clubs

I had no idea what an RSL club was when I first arrived in Oz. All I saw was a fabulous building near the beach with people buzzing around inside, all looking jolly and drinking. I immediately raced in, only to find under closer inspection, that the club was mainly made up of older people, so I slowly backed away and found out more.

Returned and Services League clubs have evolved over the years. A quick look back finds that the League was started after the 1914–1918 war by the Gallipoli Veterans and still continues to carry on with their great work.

The clubs themselves are mainly for members, but often host a variety of shows and live bands in their function rooms. They also have restaurants, bars, 'pokies' (poker machines) and satellite TV, to watch the big game on.

TOP TIP
RSL clubs can vary greatly; some are livelier than others, so just check out the one in your area before you head down there thinking you're in for a good old knees-up.

Gambler's Delight!

'Pokies' are plentiful in hotels (pubs) and social clubs. They are the most popular form of gambling in Australia and are blamed for encouraging chronic gamblers. They have even been restricted to casinos only in Western Australia. I have seen huge billboards with advertisements for overcoming your gambling addiction, so it does seem to be a problem and maybe something to be aware of if you're that way inclined!

Horse or greyhound racing is another popular pastime, and it operates using the *TAB* system (a state Totaliser Agency Board), which you see plastered on the wall of most pubs and clubs.

Melbourne Cup Day is similar to Ascot, where the ladies dress up in elegant outfits and oversized eccentric hats, but most of Australia comes to a halt that day and uses it as an excuse for a holiday and a jolly good booze up.

ODD SPOT
Aussie pubs are referred to as hotels, even though many of them don't offer accommodation!

'Keno' is another term you will see a lot of. It refers to a game that resembles bingo, but is a little more complex.

The Australian Lottery or 'Lotto' is racked with confusion. How they have managed to make a simple game like the lottery so complex, I really can't answer.

No longer can you pop into the newsagents and buy a $1 ticket, you are now bombarded with different choices of lottery games. The lottery is played five times a week on a Monday, Tuesday, Wednesday, Thursday and Saturday and there are different games for each state.

It is the same principle with regards to choosing your six numbers plus two supplements and it still costs a dollar a row. But after intense research, I have found that most games have a minimum number of rows you can purchase. Only a select few will let you buy a ticket for just one dollar as many of the games require you to purchase several rows.

So now I stick to scratchcards ('scratchies') as they are cheaper, easier and make more sense to me than the Lotto.

Australia's Frequent Festivals

Australia is host to many different festivals and carnivals. The most famous are Sydney's flamboyant Mardi Gras and Melbourne's International Comedy Festival, and their Film Festival, to name just a few.

Once again, each state has their own special celebrations for music, arts, writing, comedy and other specific themes. Some are huge and spectacular and others are smaller community-based events.

The open-air concerts have an unwritten system that most Aussies automatically fall in with:

1. Get there early on the morning of the concert – tartan rug in hand.
2. Find appropriate 'possie' (position) for watching concert.
3. Lay out tartan rug on favoured spot and secure with tent pegs.
4. Leave favoured spot/rug and carry on with normal daytime routine.
5. Return when concert is due to start with 'esky' (cool box) full of picnic food and booze to the area you previously secured.
6. Camp chairs are optional – as long as they are low, so as not to obscure the view of others sitting behind you on their tartan rug.

TOP TIP
A good idea when you are purchasing your tartan
rug for open-air concert pleasure is to buy one with
a more distinctive pattern.

Bonfire Night, No More!

Up until the late 1970s, Guy Fawkes Night was
celebrated in Oz. But as November is right at the
beginning of the summer, and therefore bushfire
season, it has been phased out.

The sale and use of fireworks is prohibited in most states and
territories, due to misuse and personal injury, so if you need
a firework fix, you will have to go along to an organised
event. These are not hard to find. There are many stunning
displays, as Australia has become quite the pyrotechnic
master.

Australia-wide Events

No one loves a party more than the Aussies, so here are
some dates for which to stock up on hangover cures:

- **January 1** – New Year's Day
- **January 26** – Australia Day
- **March/April** – Good Friday/Easter Monday
- **April 25** – ANZAC Day
- **Second Monday in June** – Queen's Birthday
  (apart from WA who celebrate it in late Sept)
- **December 25** – Christmas Day
- **December 26** – Boxing Day
  ...*except SA who instead celebrate*...
- **First work day after Christmas** – Proclamation
  Day

ODD SPOT
Although Melbourne Cup Day is a public holiday
for metropolitan Melbourne only, the whole of
Australia unofficially celebrates this event. It is
held on the first Tuesday in November and many
people go to their local racetrack to back the gee-
gees and have several drinks.

Resources

Restaurants

www.restaurant.org.au
www.bestrestaurants.com.au

Beach Safety

www.sls.com.au

Fitness Centres and Gyms

www.gymlink.com.au (to find a gym in your area)
www.fitnessfirst.com.au
www.zumba.com

RSL Clubs

www.rsl.org.au

Festivals

http://en.wikipedia.org/wiki/List_of_festivals_in_Australia

12: Driving Me Crazy!

On the face of it, driving in Australia is very much the same as driving in England, only omitting the unwritten law of common courtesy.

It's not so much recklessness that afflicts Aussies, or even road rage – they are famed for being laid back, so it's more a case of missing etiquette. The British turn-taking scenario of "after you... no really, you go first... oh, but I must insist" is not recognised as a road rule here, but I have to say once you leave your manners behind and embrace your new-found antisocial attitude, it all seems to flow perfectly, without any bunny-hopping hesitation.

Flashing your headlights at other drivers no longer indicates the other car to go first at T-junctions, etc. It actually means that you are warning oncoming traffic that they are about to approach a police speed checkpoint.

I'm extremely grateful for this change, due to a defective gene which makes me unable to differentiate between right and left, I was forever injecting a bubbly jet of windscreen-washing solution onto my windscreen and having my wipers frantically whisking away, when all I intended to do was to be kind and let someone to go before me.

My first venture onto a highway in Oz actually turned me into a dribbling idiot. The rule states 'stick to the left lane unless overtaking'. Unfortunately, I dared to overtake as I had been following a ute with flapping canvas and sharp pointy metal objects loosely bound, looking like they could break free at any moment and veer straight through my windscreen and into my neck. Within seconds I realised that my rear view mirror was taken up by a harrowing 100-tonne Kenworth truck about six inches from my tailgate. Definitely not your typical laid-back Aussie!

Once you have been driving Down Under, it is essential to get your UK licence changed to an Aussie one within three months, otherwise you could be classed as driving without a licence and therefore subject to police prosecution if caught.

Luckily, since March 2006 they have changed the rules for Brits obtaining a licence and you no longer have to take the theory test. All you need to do now is pop into your local transport office and produce your UK licence, fill in the relevant forms, pay the fee and make sure you can read the last line on the eyesight chart!

When I arrived in May 2006, I thought it was mandatory to take the theory test, and apparently the new rule hadn't filtered down to the employees of Queensland Transport either, as they readily accepted my money for the many blundered attempts at the considerably undemanding multiple-choice test that I consistently failed.

Watch Out for Pedestrians

Back on the streets, if you intend to turn either left or right when the traffic lights have turned green, then you must watch out for pedestrians as they *also* have a little green man telling them to go forth and that it's safe to cross. Frankly, I have never encountered a more dangerous sequence of turn-taking, and it took many shaken fists at poor unsuspecting children on bikes before I researched further and realised that it was *they* who had right of way, and not me. Hopefully this paragraph has saved the lives (or nerves) of thousands of children happily cycling home after their fun-packed day at school, and prevented them from being mown down by British drivers who thought they were obeying the traffic lights to perfection.

TOP TIP

Another point about traffic lights is that if you are first in the queue, be really aware of watching for them to change. The usual red... red-amber... green sequence is now more of an abrupt red... GREEN! So be alert.

Persistent Petrol Fluctuations

As we all know, petrol prices normally vary from garage to garage (known here as 'servo') on average a penny or two? Well, in Australia the petrol prices vary all day. You can go into your local Woolworth's supermarket and see the price on the way in, and get on with your grocery shopping, thinking you will fill up with fuel on the way out. But by the time you get out you will notice that the price has now changed, only a little but nonetheless annoying, as now there are double the amount of people queuing to get their petrol. And that's not the worst of it. The prices change dramatically from day to day. After much analysis of this peculiar practice, I have come across a pattern which I think you may find useful – or you may want to just mock me for being such a nerd.

- **Monday morning** has high petrol prices, for instance $1.45
- **Monday afternoon** the price generally falls to around $1.41
- **Tuesday** and **Wednesday** are the best days to fill up, as the price is about $1.38 (but everyone

else seems to know the secret and also wants to fill up, so take a book with you – preferably this one)

- **Thursday** and **Friday** are generally higher
- **Sunday** the price drops a little.

It really is an odd phenomenon to get used to, and most Aussies think that this is just normal, that it happens all over the world. Apparently, this has been the case for a number of years as *allegedly* all government departments that paid pensions to people (such as the old-age pension, war-veteran's pension, job search benefit etc) were paid to everyone on Thursday. In addition, most workers got paid on a Thursday or Friday, so it was widely assumed that they would put the prices up when they knew people had money in their bank accounts. True or not, the Aussies aren't complaining, so why should we?

ODD SPOT
The legal minimum driving age in most states is 17 apart from in Victoria where it is 18 and in South Australia where it is 16!

How to Park a Car – Aussie Style!

Free parking is available in Australia, barring airports and hospitals. Unlike Essex where I was horrified to discover that I had to pay and display at my local Somerfield store, even when I was just popping in for a pint of milk and some peanut M&M's. You are reimbursed when you show the other half of your ticket at the checkout, but that really isn't the point; it's extremely inconvenient and if you don't have a 20p coin on you, you're buggered and forced to shop elsewhere.

Anyway, all you have to do here in Oz is observe the clear signs that tell you how long you can park and on which days.

Car park bays are spacious and you no longer have to squeeze carefully out of your car to avoid banging into the car next to you with your door. The child parking bays are ridiculously oversized and you feel unworthy of using them unless you have a minimum of three children, a dog, two goats and a couple of loose chickens.

Reverse angle parking seems to crop up on occasion – but this varies from state to state. If you do come across these type of bays, never park nose in first – you will be frowned and tutted at, but only by Australians. Most poms will recognise you as a newbie fellow expat and wonder over to introduce themselves.

One rule that must be obeyed, which is *totally* different from England, is that you can only park your car on the road the way the traffic is flowing. So you can no longer eagerly hop across to the other side of the road when you spy a space. You must first turn around and then go into it. Otherwise you may face a fine and even some penalty points.

All in all, the good news is that once you become more open, accept the new ways and read the Highway Code, driving in Australia is no longer petrifying, but a pleasure

Buying a Car in Oz

Cars in Australia seem to hold their value a lot more than in the UK. You also see cars that you haven't seen since the 70s trundling around, which is a bit weird. Before I came over, I was told that there was no MOT on cars and all Aussies drive around in old bangers. How glad I was to find out that this was an untruth.

It is true, there is no MOT, but in some states vehicles must have a *Certificate of Roadworthiness* (or a

'Roadworthy') before they are sold, and used vehicles before they are reregistered.

A 'roadworthy' doesn't necessarily guarantee the car's mechanical reliability, (you must get a separate vehicle inspection from the RAC – or similar – for that) but it does ensure that the vehicle is safe for normal road use, as it has been tested by a licensed vehicle tester.

Once you have your roadworthy, you must then get yourself some *Compulsory Third Party insurance* (CTP).

CTP is a legal requirement throughout Australia. If an accident were to happen and the driver had no CTP, then they may find themselves financially liable for the damages paid to anyone who is injured. They would also have a hefty fine to pay for being unregistered, as you cannot have a registration certificate (see below) without it.

CTP covers you for personal injury caused by other insured drivers and also for claims made against you from other road users. It doesn't cover you for damage to other vehicles.

You must prove that you have CTP (by way of a green slip from the insurance company) before you can get your vehicle registered. This is transferred to the new owner of the vehicle when you sell it.

Once you have those two items ticked off, it's time to get your certificate of registration ('rego') to be displayed on the inside of the windscreen of your vehicle and renewed annually. The cost of 'rego' varies from state to state; it depends on your engine size, but it includes road tax, stamp duty and CTP.

CTP is the absolute minimum insurance requirement and most car owners have separate insurance cover as well. Insurance companies are pretty much the same as in the UK and you can still choose from 'third party fire and theft' and 'fully comprehensive'.

TOP TIP

In quirky Queensland, some cars advertise the word "interested?" on the back of their cars. You'll be forgiven for thinking they are trying to advertise a seedy establishment of some kind. In fact, it is a legal loophole whereby the owner is trying to avoid officially advertising the car for sale by avoiding the phrase "for sale" – as some council districts are against this type of advertising.

Stamp Duty on Vehicles

Stamp duty varies considerably on vehicles; it has to be paid on all car purchases and it is tiered anywhere from 1% to 6.5% depending on the individual state and the value of the car.

TOP TIP

If you buy a car from a dealer for over $57,466, you will also have to pay luxury car tax on top of the stamp duty, but if you buy the car privately, you will not have to pay this tax.

Transferring Your No Claims Discount

When you arrive in Oz, make sure you have your no claims discount proof with you, as opposed to having it all bundled up with your other paperwork somewhere on the seven seas.

ODD SPOT

No claims discount is also known as rating 1 if you have 65% no claims, going down in increments to rating 5 if you have 0% no claims bonus.

When we applied for car insurance in Queensland, we fully expected to have to show them proof of our no-claims history, by way of a letter from our previous insurers. It made no odds to our new insurers, who let it be known to us that our insurance could be void if it became apparent that we had a poor driving history that we hadn't disclosed, in the event of a claim.

Check online to see what regulations the car insurance companies use in your state, so you can either be baffled or armed with the appropriate paper work.

Quick Transport Translations

Australian	English
Servo	Petrol station
Kombi	Van-like vehicle
Wagon (or station wagon)	Estate-type car
KPL	Kilometres per litre
Ute	Utility vehicle
Dual-cab Ute	Utility vehicle with extra seating (typically seats five)
Park	Car parking space

Resources

Renting a Vehicle

www.avis.com.au
www.budget.com.au
www.europcar.com.au
www.hertz.com.au
www.thrifty.com.au

Buying a Vehicle

www.redbook.com.au
www.carsales.com.au
www.bikesales.com.au
www.carpoint.com.au
www.countrycars.com.au

Car Insurance

www.nrma.com.au/carinsurance
www.budgetdirect.com.au
www.allianz.com.au/car-insurance
www.aami.com.au

13: Miscellaneous Matters

Utility Calamity

After the first six months of using my washing machine I started to find that my clothes were coming out of the wash covered in small, dark brown flakes.

Thinking it was mould of some type, Max cleaned out all the pipes and ran bleach through the machine. This cleared it for a short time, but within a few months it returned and I was once again shaking my clothes furiously in the backyard trying hard not to let these annoying flakes venture into the pool.

A short time later we had some friends round for a 'barbie'. My friend was looking at me in a suspicious manner while I was once again flinging my clothes frantically about and pegging them onto the line. Then she walked over to me, very cautiously to avoid me taking an eye out, and gave me some golden information: Because many washing cycles are performed on low temperate settings, say 40°C, your machine doesn't always get a good clear out. So every now and again you should run a really hot wash, just to keep it free from stagnant particles.

My washing machine was quite bad, so I did have to run about three hot cycles, but considering I was about to call in an expensive plumber, I think this is a great tip!

ODD SPOT

Bathwater drains away anti-clockwise down the plughole, but not all the time! It depends on many other dynamics, like how many kids are in the bath, or toys and apparently if the plumber put the plughole in correctly. So, there seems to be no answer to this myth.

Football Crazy

Soccer is what Aussies call English football, whereas football (the Australian variety) is a bloody battlefield where hulking men wear extremely tight, small pants and hug a rugby ball.

There's probably more to it than that, but I'm no expert on the subject and so am not at liberty to divulge further information.

Just make sure you put little Johnny in the right sport, or he may be heading for a toothless homecoming.

Hot Phone Tip

If you using an *Optus* telephone exchange (provider), the 1471 equivalent to find out the number of the person who last called you *10#. But you will be charged for this call.

A 'call waiting' service means that if a second caller phones you while you are already talking on the phone, you will hear a series of beeps and you can ask the first caller to hold while you answer the second caller.

This is similar to the service in the UK but remember here, the second caller doesn't know that you are already on the phone as it simply rings and rings as if no one is home. There is no polite little voice explaining:

"Please hold the line, the other caller knows you are waiting."

We got rid of our 'call waiting' service, and bought an answer machine instead.

Loo with a View

Now I can't vouch for the whole of Australia, but of the public lavatories I have visited in several different states, a disturbing amount of them have a gap of about three to four millimetres between the door and the doorframe. I always find this extremely annoying and a complete invasion of privacy. I am just waiting for the day that an inquisitive pre-schooler wails like a banshee after peeking through the gap and witnesses a hovering bottom changing a tampon.

Metric-mania

Australia officially went metric in 1972 in primary schools, then later in secondary schools and slowly into all the different industries until 1988. They now work in kilometres, metres, grams and centimetres, so it may be an idea to have a quick revision session on this before you enter the country, as telling someone you weigh "nine stone five" and are "five foot six" will probably be met with a baffled look by anyone under the age of 30.

Posting to the Poms

Australia Post has practically the same range of services as the Royal Mail, only the counter staff are generally happier to see you and far more helpful.

When you post parcels to the UK, you must take identification (such as a driver's licence) with you to the post office, as they need to identify you for customs reasons.

They will take down your licence number and you are required to fill in a customs slip (Customs Douane CN22.) On one half you must supply your name, address, and phone number; on the other half a detailed description of the contents *and* the value of the parcel … so bang goes the surprise for the recipient!

TOP TIP

While you are in Australia Post, ask your assistant if you can have some of the customs slips – that way you can fill them in at home the next time you have a parcel. This saves time in the queue at the post office and makes the whole process a lot more streamlined.

One other thing: the post is only delivered once a day and on Mondays through to Fridays only – not on Saturdays. You no longer have the luxury of a letterbox in your front door; instead your post will be nestled into your mailbox on or around your front drive by a brightly clad motorcyclist who bears no resemblance to Postman Pat.

Daylight Cravings

The term 'daylight savings' of course refers to putting the clocks back, or forward. But, because Australia is such an enormous landmass, they have three different time zones:

EST (Eastern Standard Time) is used in ACT, NSW, QLD, TAS and VIC. EST is **10 hours ahead** of GMT. During daylight savings this becomes **11 hours ahead** – except QLD who doesn't join in.

CST (Central Standard Time) is used in SA and NT. CST is **9.5 hours ahead** of GMT. On daylight savings, SA is **10.5 hours ahead** of GMT but NT doesn't join in.

WST (Western Standard Time) is used in Western Australia. WST is **8 hours ahead** of GMT. WA was on a trial daylight savings for three years, but this has now been rejected.

In 2008 a new referendum for daylight savings was introduced. TAS, VIC, SA, NSW and ACT all start daylight savings on the first Sunday of October and finish on the first Sunday in April.

NT, QLD and again WA, don't partake of the modern daylight savings ritual, so they don't get the luxury of having an extra hour of daylight in the summer. This means even when it's been scorching hot all day in Brisbane, the sun still goes down by 6.45pm in the height of summer – and the dawn chorus starts at 4.50am.

Plastic Fantastic

Australia's bank notes are made of plastic!

Well, actually, they are made of polymer. The first note was introduced in 1988 and then by 1996, Australia became the first country in the world to have a complete set of polymer notes. To this day, Australia is still the only country with the technology for these notes, so any country around the world with polymer bank notes, will have licensed them from Australia.

The great advantage of having them is that they are far more durable than the old paper types, lasting up to four times as long.

They are also harder to duplicate; a little window in the notes makes scanning and photocopying difficult, therefore providing greater security.

But the main bonus of having plastic notes is you needn't worry if you leave one in your pocket and it goes through the wash – it just comes out clean and not all chewed up!

TOP TIP

If you fancy catching a wave, you don't have to worry about taking a wallet or bag with you on the beach, simply take a few notes in your pocket!

Winter Drawers On

I was shocked and amazed when I first moved to Australia, when I read on the front of one of the local newspapers: "Volunteers battled in the freezing winds in an attempt to finish the botanical garden in time for the grand opening."

You may not see anything wrong with this headline, but believe me, when I arrived in mid-winter, the air temperature was probably no less than 18°C. To read the words "freezing winds" made me guffaw.

Yet a funny thing happened. After a full year of what I can loosely describe as 'seasons', another winter was upon us. As the winter drew on, I started to find myself becoming increasingly chilly. It started with just having to pop on a cardy, but then it escalated to searching through my clothing archive for a warm coat, and Heaven forbid, a scarf.

I had acclimatised! And the reason I am telling you about it is so you don't sell/give/throw away your winter woollies before you move over. I did, and how I long for my stylish *Next* jumpers, my Marks & Spencer boots and my faux fur-lined jacket. You may only need them for a couple of months, but it is so refreshing to wear different clothes, to snuggle up and be cosy – and perhaps even get your hot-water bottle out at night.

Of course this all depends on where you are going to live in Australia. If you are going to head up to far north Queensland, I doubt you will get much use out of them, but if you're heading for Victoria (four seasons in one day country) then bag 'em up and bring 'em.

TOP TIP

If you do forget to pack your warm boots, don't panic; you can always buy yourself a fair dinkum pair of Aussie Ugg boots. Oooh, the luxury!

Back in time?

I once got chatting to my neighbour, a friendly elderly gentleman, as he was edging the grass along his front path with some sort of metal contraption. Having experienced many frustrations with my electric whipper snipper (strimmer to us), I asked him if I could have a go with his edger. He kindly agreed and handed it over, before adding, "All the Victorians use these, you know."

"Wow, you've looked after it well," I innocently answered.

But of course, as soon as I'd said that, I realised he meant people from the state of Victoria as opposed to 18th-century gardeners.

Down Under Dialect

Don't be alarmed by how Australians start their sentences. It's nearly always with the words "look" or "listen". This immediately holds your attention as you think they may be mildly annoyed with you about something you have said.

But then, as the sentence unfolds, you realise that they weren't annoyed, it probably wasn't even of high importance and in fact it could be a triviality.

Queenslanders have yet another trait: even before they start with the look/listen onset, they slowly let out an "Arr" noise, which sounds not unlike a very loud and frightening crow.

Although some Aussie words are pronounced a little differently, you can generally understand what they mean. The problem comes when you start conversing with someone from New Zealand. I have many lovely Kiwi friends, but sometimes for the life of me, I can't comprehend what they are saying.

It seems as though they have taken the normal use of vowels and completely scrambled them up to make a completely new word. A classic example is their pronunciation of the number six, which they pronounce "sex".

I will let you draw your own conclusion about Kiwi English. Just be warned that if they mention that they have a "huge dick", they are undoubtedly referring to their over-proportioned outside entertaining area, so don't take offence.

The Aussies have a great many unusual expressions that you may find amusing. Some you may have heard on the TV; others you will no doubt come across in general conversation.

It's the ones that are used on a daily basis that I find infectious, like the use of the word "hey" as a sentence starter ("hey, did you know..?").

I do draw the line at letting my sentences veer up at the end in a questioning way; it sounds fine when the locals do it, but truly painful when copied by the Brits.

An expression I love to hear is "too easy". What a positive statement *that* is. I remember when the removal men were bringing our new top-loader washing machine into the house and were inquiring as to the whereabouts of the laundry room.

When directed they both said in unison, "Too easy!" I have adopted that phrase ever since, although I accept that no doubt it sounds rather pompous in my English accent.

Other day-to-day expressions are "heaps" (instead of "loads") and "I'm so over it" when you have had enough of something.

Children are mainly encouraged to "hop" (into the car or up to the table). Of course I do not mean they are forced to jump about on one leg.

Most of these phrases are great and I am pleased to fall in with them. Unfortunately there are a couple that are not quite so catchy.

In certain situations, it is not uncommon for Aussies to substitute the word "though" with "but"... Here's an example:

"He can't dance. He sings well, though," as we put it, would be:

"He can't dance. He sings well, but."

It takes a little while to get used to this, and some of my English friends (in particular an English teacher I know) cringe and find it unbearable!

Another common misuse of a word is "youse" as in, the plural of you. This brings me neatly onto the world of Aussie pronunciation.

Aussie Pronunciation

Word	How Aussies say it
Project	*Prow-ject*
Yoghurt	*Yow-gurt*
Vitamin	*Vite-a-min*
CV	Resumé (pronounced *rezz-yew-may* or *rejsh-a-may*)
Auction	Ock-tion
Data	Dahta
maroon (the colour)	Mur-ow-n
Debut	Day-boo

ODD SPOT

One other little misunderstanding is the use of the word Durex. It is not used in the manner with which we are acquainted in the UK, but it is a brand name they used to use for adhesive tape. I bet that made your eyes water!

Aussie Phrases

Word/Phrase	What it means
Don't come the raw prawn	Don't try and fool me
Flat out like a lizard drinking	As fast as possible
A go-er	Something that will definitely happen
Keen as mustard	Enthusiastic
Shoot through	To leave rather quickly
Bail out	To leave
Cut lunch	Sandwiches

Wag	To play truant
Rock-up	To turn up
Ripper	Great
Rapt	Very happy/delighted
Beaut	Very good
Dinkie die	The whole truth
Fair Dinkum	Honest/genuine
O-S	Overseas
Spunk	Good-looking (sexy)
Strides/daks	Trousers
Smoko	Cigarette break or tea break
Shout	To buy a round of drinks

Other daily phrases

Phrase	What it means
Tradie (tray-dee)	Tradesperson
Garbo	Rubbish-bin collector
Journo	Journalist
Milko	Milkman
Salvos	Salvation army
Kiwi or Enzedder	Person from New Zealand
Galah	Idiot
Hoon	Hooligan
Dag	Lump of dirt or faeces entangled with wool hanging from sheep's bottom. Mildly abusive term!
Ocker	Rough Aussie person

14: Straight from the Horse's Mouth

I am still constantly amazed by the many British people I meet with their own story of why they decided to move over here, and how at one point or another, they wished they hadn't. After collating all the information in this book, some of it from newbies straight off the boat and some from experienced settlers well into their twentieth year, it occurred to me that while the stories they told are all very different, the message is the same:

Don't give in to your homesickness; give your new life a fair go.

I have included real-life inspirational stories from many of the people who have crossed my path while writing this book. I hope that when you have made your journey and inevitably start to feel the pangs of homesickness, you can relate to some of them and realise you are not alone, and that it *will* pass.

My Nirvana by Sam Mallinder

Our little adventure began a few years ago in 2004. We left the grey skies of Sheffield and set off on an adventure to live overseas in New Zealand.

The South Island of New Zealand, we soon discovered, could be as grey as England but with the added problem of cold houses to boot. My God, you don't realise what a fantastic invention central heating is until you have to live in a wooden house without it!

In 2006 it came to our attention that my husband's chosen career path would pay dividends and allow us the privilege of moving to Australia and experiencing the warmer climate we thought we would have experienced in NZ! We took the opportunity to live in Oz. We hit the ground running and picked out the house of our dreams after only a few days.

Life in Australia seemed to be a lot more social – the weather will do that for you! We were happy bunnies all round. The kids settled quickly into their new school. I did my bit and volunteered in the classroom – anything to give the credit cards a rest from the shopping malls. I met some lovely people, mostly in the same boat: new arrivals from either interstate or overseas. Day-to-day living was pretty good.

But it happens when you least expect it. It creeps into your headspace and it's hard to shake – missing people, that is. Missing family and friends and the familiarity of your old life. It became a regular conversation point in our household of how and when we could afford to make a trip back to Blighty. I was beginning to feel a true desire to show off my two children to their extended family. Phone calls and web chats with the folks back home became more frequent and at times I was fraught with absolute jealousy if I heard of any of my friends having family visiting them.

And then I was served a curved ball. On the night of the Melbourne Cup 2007 (another huge social event where ladies can dress up and gather together to chat and drink bubbly), I was reading to my son in bed when the phone rang. My daughter answered it and announced that there was a woman on the phone with a strange accent. I giggled to myself knowing it would be someone from the UK and that her native tongue sounded strange to her after living so far away for so long out of her short life. At this point I intercepted the call that would change all our plans and conversations about when we would travel back to the UK. It was the call any person would dread. A call to tell me that my dad had been found dead in his flat.

My head went into free fall and I had the terrible task of having to tell my sisters that our dad had died. They both still live in Sheffield. Social services had found a letter in his flat that linked him back to me and bypassed his other daughters who lived only miles away. My support network here in Australia kicked into overdrive. Girlfriends rallied to help. I began the task of ringing airlines to organise a flight back to the UK. I had read somewhere on the internet that airlines offer compassionate fares in such circumstances. I can tell you now that such a thing does not exist! Before I knew it I was saying goodbye to my husband and kids and was on a flight to Manchester. My emotions were mixed: I was excited to see the people I had been pining for and dreading the responsibility I was returning home to. I was also scared of what I would feel like once I landed back in the UK. Would this trip open a can of worms and shatter our life in Australia? Would the desire to be amongst my loved ones again make me want to pack our things up in Australia and run back to the comforts of home?

The reunion was phenomenal. I don't think I have ever been squeezed so tight. It was poignant to see that time stands still for no one. In person I could witness the lines that had appeared around my mother's eyes that were disguised in photographs or in images seen over the webcam. My nieces and nephews had grown so tall. My heart broke to know that I would only be with them for a week (as that was all I could bear to be apart from my own children).

So I had one week. One week to say hello and goodbye. One week to secretly assess whether I would want to return to England to live.

I was dragged on a shopping spree to be loaded down with gifts from my family to take back to Australia with me. I was teased unmercifully for my Aussie twang – speak to any of my Australian friends and they would laugh hysterically at the idea of my accent being compared to theirs! I was confused by the English currency – seeing coins again after using Eftpos for so long. I was perplexed at the self-service supermarket, as I was so used to having my bags packed for me by a chirpy teenager asking how my day had been. I couldn't get over how cold the wind was. I was shaken to the core to contemplate how we could ever go back to living in such small spaces and driving on such narrow roads. As much as I took a lot of comfort from the familiarity of being home I realised that my home was no longer in Sheffield. Though saying goodbye again was heartbreaking and painful I felt I had found my nirvana in Australia: a place I hope to share with my family and friends should they ever to choose to visit.

Australian Horizons by Mary Morgan

I would say first of all, in my defence, that it really wasn't my idea to move to Oz. In fact, the idea wasn't even on the radar. Through a series of reshuffles, shake-ups, and sideways expansions, my husband was unexpectedly offered a position in his firm's Australian branch. He was keen – very keen – and got our two children pretty well fired up too.

He got all the books and CDs promoting Australia he could lay his hands on and I had to admit it did seem very nice – all that blue sky and endless sun! I began to imagine it as being a bit like our Spanish summer holidays but better, because the locals would be English-speaking – sort of.

In the end he convinced me that it would be:

A healthy life for our son and daughter.

A marvellous climate where he (work permitting) could play golf all year round.

A relaxing lifestyle for me, where I could learn to play golf too and we could spend more time together.

And then the clincher... We'd have a large, modern villa-type home (twice the size we could afford in the UK) with a huge swimming pool.

My sisters were dumbfounded at first as we were a very united family, living in close proximity to each other. But the more my husband talked about the sun and sea the more they began to think that Christmas holidays in the warmth of Australia would be an excellent idea! They would definitely be over to see us; in fact so many of our friends were inviting themselves over that I began to worry about accommodating everyone.

So the day came when we packed up our furniture, and all our belongings and said, "Farewell, see you soon in Oz!"

After only a few weeks, however, I felt we had definitely made the wrong decision. Australia is NOT a bigger England with sun. I think it was easier for my husband and children. They settled in at work and school, making friends quite quickly.

My husband was introduced at the local golf club within the first week! He couldn't understand how lonely and cut off I felt. I was stuck in a furnished flat all day with no one to talk to. Living here is NOT like *Neighbours*, people do not bob in and out of each other's houses all the time!

To tell the truth, although they speak English here, it took me a long time to understand the accent, and worse, they looked puzzled when *I* spoke, as if I came from a foreign country, which of course, although I didn't realise it at the time, I did! I was losing confidence fast, so to boost myself a bit, I tried to keep things the same as at home.

I shopped for UK products, or as near as I could get. I bought only English magazines and would cook the same style meals as before, although they tasted different here. I felt that if I could keep things the same, I would still be me. Oh yes, I was fighting Australia!

We bought a huge house with a pool but my lovely furniture, which had been so carefully crated up, looked all wrong! Some china had not survived the journey and some electrical goods would not work at all! I sat and cried. From the letters I received it was clear that everybody at home had forgotten about holidays with us, deciding after all that it was too far and settling for sunny spots in the Caribbean or adventurous ski trips with parties of *our* friends instead. I wanted to go home. Everyone wanted us back, promising lovely outings and holidays together. I was crying non-stop by now and in the end my husband agreed. We were going home.

I was so happy despite losing huge amounts of money on the sale of the cars and house; despite my husband's lost promotion; despite going from a huge villa with a pool to a two-bedroom rental (just for the moment). I radiated happiness. I was looking forward to picking up my life with family and friends just where I had left off.

But the first excitement of returning quickly evaporated. Everyone was incredibly casual about meeting up – as if we had just got off the number 7 bus, rather than come from halfway around the world. The gap we left had been filled, they had got on with their lives. But the biggest shock was the change in me. I had fought against Australia but my experience had opened my horizons without me realising.

It was time for a reality check: nothing stays the same. People and circumstances change all the time. But we had changed far more than the folks at home. Without wanting to, I had experienced and seen things that had changed me and nothing could alter that. In my homesickness I had wanted to go back to a place that existed only in my memories. The reality was that everything seemed smaller, more crowded and far less inviting than in my imagination. I had nearly destroyed my family, ruined my husband's career and wasted a huge chunk of our life savings.

What did I learn from this expensive lesson? Don't compare countries! Australia isn't an English Spain or a sunny UK! It's unique, a one-off, it's Australia! Give yourself time, at the very *least* 18 months, to acclimatise. It's not going to happen in less. Before you arrive, don't build up impossible expectations. Great things are possible in Oz but often you are your own worst obstacle – look at what happened to me and try not to look back. Yesterday can be reached again only in your memories. Memories are good to have but, as I have found out, that is what they are, memories.

For the past 15 years I have changed my outlook, to have experiences, because we have been very lucky. We had the opportunity to start over again in Australia and I have not looked back for a moment. We get maximum value out of every day and no, this time I did not take the furniture!

Urban Woman by Raylene Clarke

My story is a bit different because I am actually Australian. When I was asked to write down my experiences I thought, *Hang on a bit; I'm not one of those poms, forever yo-yoing back and forth across the world!*

Then I thought again and it struck me that maybe I am, only in reverse (I currently live in London).

I'm a city girl. I was born in Medinde; an eastern suburb of Adelaide. It's a pretty nice suburb, although I never really thought about it too much when I was growing up.

It was just home to me, my mum, dad and five brothers. Anyway, the reason I'm talking about Medinde was just to let you know that I really am an urban creature.

Everyone over here in 'Pommie Land' thinks that because I'm an Aussie I know all about the bush, cattle musters and sheep shearing. Well I don't, I wouldn't have a clue. It's not that I am a particularly ignorant person, it's just a fact that most of us Aussies live in cities. All we know about the Great Outback and such, we have learnt from programmes on the telly. The closest I have been to a sheep is roasted on the table at mum's...

What I am trying to say is, these are Aussie stereotypes – as are kangaroos hopping down the main street. It is true, we are outdoor types though; with our summer climate it would be hard not to be. I'm sure that if England had the same sort of weather everyone would be outside too. But when the winter comes most people like to snuggle up and sit by a cosy fire.

It's not that we have some mad gene that makes us rush outside regardless — like everywhere else it just depends on the weather. Oh, there's another myth too: Australia does have a winter, unless you go up north to the tropics where it's ...well, tropical!

My partner, Jason, comes from a similar urban background. Being a man, it's been more difficult for him over here, not conforming to the typical Aussie male image I mean. Our pommie friends think he should spend his weekends croc wrestling and parading around in a Driza-Bone full length wax jacket, with a Bushman's hat on his head. But no, he is a banker!

We met on campus at Adelaide Uni and it was lust at first sight, but we have been together for more than 12 years now, so I guess you could say we are pretty much an item.

Aussies are really walkabout artists, so when we announced to our respective families that we intended to move to London to further our careers, no one turned a hair. To be honest it wasn't so much furthering our careers — "we had done the math" as the Americans say — and we had worked out the fairly obvious; every pound sterling earned was worth two Aussie dollars, more or less. Therefore we could save twice as fast. What we didn't take into consideration was that London was probably twice as expensive to live in as Adelaide!

We have been here for about nine years now and we certainly enjoy London, but we do yo-yo. During holidays and between work contracts we are off! What always strikes me is how empty Australia is. How clean and bright it is: a *staggering* brightness. With fresh produce, clean air, unpolluted sea and sky, Australia almost sounds like a fitness farm!

After a few days we take it for granted again and then find ourselves amazed on our return to find the London streets so crowded: a shoving heaving mass of humanity stuck in long, long grey winters. Then we start the daily round of a working life and slowly readapt.

But seven months ago we had a big wake-up call. Out of the blue I was hospitalised for a couple of weeks. It was a pretty scary experience. Don't get me wrong, the staff were, for the most part, absolutely fantastic and I am hugely grateful to them, but I just couldn't believe the conditions they have to work in.

Jason and I both agreed that it was modern-world nursing and drugs, but in a Developing World hospital. The building itself was grim to say the least; rather like a converted workhouse or something equally depressing. The corridors were piled high with stuff, of what specific nature I'm not sure.

The thing is we really want to start a family in the near future, and like all prospective parents, we want to do the best we possibly can for our baby. I don't want to repeat that workhouse experience if I can help it... And I *can* help it.

Anytime now we will sell our lovely little flat (that cost a small fortune) and what is left after the mortgage guys have been paid off will be our nest egg for starting out in Oz. I do love our life in London. It's an exciting city where we have great friends and great times but we are moving forward, like our friends, ready to develop a different stage in our lives.

Living life is about moving forward, doing and being the best you can. I can't imagine a better or healthier life for my children than running free on the clean white beaches of Adelaide, under sunny skies.

Someone at work said to me, "Won't you feel sad, saying goodbye to all your friends here?" Well, the answer is, I have no intention of *saying* "goodbye".

This isn't the age of the sailing ship, when it took six or more weeks to reach Australia. The world becomes increasingly small, I am glad to say, especially when it comes to friendship.

I still have most of my uni friends and we keep in touch fairly regularly. I have found phone cards and emails very handy for a quick gossip! I don't see why it will be any different with my London friends.

We really are blessed these days I think, because as Jason says, no one is further away than your phone. I love that idea.

And Finally...

I have come across this quote a couple of times since I started writing this book, and I thought it so appropriate:

"No matter where you go, there <u>you</u> are."

If you found you were unhappy with certain situations in the UK, you'll probably find that you will still have matters arising in Oz that you aren't happy with. Somehow though, problems always seem to feel better in the sunshine, unless you have photosensitivity of course.

What I am trying to say, in a very roundabout English way is: be realistic about your Aussie adventure. Try not to start off by becoming a whinging pom; don't compare everything to back home and try and embrace Australia for what it really is: Australia.

I'll leave you with this last story – it happened just a few months ago...

I had been walking along the beautiful coastal boardwalk, by the sea near our home. I got chatting to a fellow Brit along the way, who told me he had experienced many problems settling in when he first arrived several years ago. So I asked him the big question: had he ever seriously thought about moving back to the UK?

He paused for a moment with his head down, then breathed in a long, deep lungful of air, opened his arms wide as if to fully behold the glorious beach in front of us, and said, "I'd rather gnaw my own leg off."

I rest my case.

About Vicky Gray

Vicky Gray grew up in Merseyside before moving with her family to Essex at the age of 13. Unbeknown to her, this relocation (although traumatic for a stroppy red-haired teenager) was to be the beginning of her passion for experiencing new places and understanding the subtle differences that make somewhere unique.

Vicky has had two successful careers. She was head nurse at dental surgeries in Essex and Harley Street before qualifying as a podiatrist in 1999.

During this time, she took as much time as possible to go off adventuring: around Europe with an absurd budget of £7 a day; backpacking around America using airports as hotels, and visiting Australia, where she knew immediately she wanted to settle.

It wasn't until finally emigrating to Australia in 2006 with her husband and three children, that the desire to write about the many bizarre and often unnerving encounters became a reality. After writing articles in *Australia & New Zealand magazine* (Merricks Media Ltd) Vicky got a publishing deal for her how-to book on the calamities of relocating and is now working on this exciting new career!

Seven Things You Never Knew About Vicky

1. Vicky once worked in a factory, applying waterproof tape onto the underside of tent seams with a steam press. She left after four days to work at a warehouse in an industrial estate selling oversized clothes, which she left after two days.

2. Vicky has an uncanny ability to untie bothersome knots.

3. In her early twenties, Vicky was often mistaken for Nicole Kidman, but as the years have gone on, she has more readily been mistaken for Charlie Dimmock.

4. Vicky's real name is Sarah, as her parents decided to change it when she was a few weeks old. Unfortunately they never officially changed it, which has been a constant source of confusion at doctors' surgeries all her life.

5. When Vicky was ten, she wrote out an entire episode of *The Young Ones* in script form, then enticed her fellow pupils to perform it at assembly.

6. Vicky is also a talented artist. She once set up a company painting children's bedroom walls, called Magical Murals.

7. Vicky once had to spend several months visiting a speech therapist, as her vocal chords had developed nodules due to singing at karaoke.

Visit Vicky's blog for articles, advice, updates and beautiful full-colour photographs at
www.australiauncovered.com

Bibliography

CultureShock! Australia by Ilsa Sharp. Published by Graphic Arts Centre Publishing Company. ISBN: 978-1-55868-0944

Frommer's Australia 2009 by Marc Llewellyn, Ron Crittall and Lee Atkinson. Published by John Wiley & Sons.ISBN: 978-0470345443

Down Under by Bill Bryson. Published by Black Swan. ISBN: 978-0552997034

Australia & New Zealand Magazine — the UK's only magazine dedicated to Down Under. Filled with unbiased and informative articles for travellers and migrants. *www.australiamagazine.co.uk*

SUNSHINE
SOUP

NOURISHING THE GLOBAL SOUL

Jo Parfitt